BOWLING

GOODYEAR
Physical Activities Series

Edited by J. Tillman Hall

Archery	Jean A. Barrett *California State University, Fullerton*
Badminton	James Poole *California State University, Northridge*
Bowling	Norman E. Showers *Southern Illinois University, Edwardsville*
Fencing	Nancy L. Curry *Southwest Missouri State College*
Folk Dance	J. Tillman Hall *University of Southern California*
Golf	Edward F. Chui *University of Hawaii*
Handball	Pete Tyson *University of Texas*
Men's Basketball	Richard H. Perry *University of Southern California*
Men's Gymnastics	Gordon Maddux *California State University, Los Angeles*
Paddleball and Racquetball	A. William Fleming *Florida International University* Joel A. Bloom *University of Houston*
Soccer	John Callaghan *University of Southern California*
Social Dance	John G. Youmans *Temple University*

Swimming	Donald L. Gambril *Harvard University*
Fundamentals of Physical Education	J. Tillman Hall *University of Southern California*
	Kenneth C. Lersten *University of Southern California*
	Merril J. Melnick *University of Southern California*
	Talmage W. Morash *California State University, Northridge*
	Richard H. Perry *University of Southern California*
	Robert A. Pestolesi *California State University, Long Beach*
	Burton Seidler *California State University, Los Angeles*
Volleyball	Randy Sandefur *California State University, Long Beach*
Tennis	Barry C. Pelton *University of Houston*
Women's Basketball	Ann Stutts *California State University, Northridge*
Women's Gymnastics	Mary L. Schreiber *California State University, Los Angeles*

GOODYEAR PUBLISHING COMPANY, INC.
Pacific Palisades, California

Goodyear Physical Activities Series
J. Tillman Hall: *Series Editor*

Norman E. Showers
*Southern Illinois University,
Edwardsville*

SECOND EDITION

BOWLING

Acknowledgments

Many thanks to my wife for her assistance and to Robert Showers and Richard Gerber for permitting the use of the bowling research. Special gratitude to Mrs. Mary P. Meyer, R.N., for her drawings. Special thanks to my students, Cheryl and Dennis Wilschetz, who performed so ably for the university photographer, Charles Cox, and his assistant, Pam Sidener. My thanks also to the university lanes manager, Earl Extrom, and his assistant, Lee Frantz, and to Robert Guelker, Intramural Director. My special thanks to Dr. Zadia Herrold, Chairman, Physical Education Department, Southern Illinois University, Edwardsville.

BOWLING
Norman E. Showers
Second Edition

Copyright © 1973, 1969 by
GOODYEAR PUBLISHING COMPANY, INC.
Pacific Palisades, California

Library of Congress Catalog Card Number: 72-90981

Current printing (last number):
10 9 8 7 6 5 4

ISBN: 0-87620-118-4
Y-1184-4
Printed in the United States of America
cover photo by Zimbel for AMF from Monkmeyer

Editor's note

The Goodyear Publishing Company presents a series of physical education books written by instructors expert in their respective fields.

These books on major sports are intended as supplementary material for the instructor and to aid the student in the understanding and mastery of the sport of his choice. Each book covers its fundamentals—the beginning techniques, rules and customs, equipment and terms—and gives to the reader the spirit of the sport.

Each author of this series brings to the reader the knowledge and skill he has acquired over many years of teaching and coaching. We sincerely hope that these books will prove invaluable to the college student or any student of the sport.

In BOWLING, Norman Showers describes the basic techniques and analyzes the fundamentals a student must master in order to become an accomplished bowler. From his experience at Southern Illinois University, Dr. Showers brings the student a comprehensive analysis of how to choose the ball, the proper stance, the pushaway, the approach, type of delivery, and aiming techniques. Terminology, objectives, scoring, and improving the game are described in detail throughout sections of the text. The finer points of bowling, playing the lane, and playing the angles are covered as are all league bowling guidelines with which the student can analyze his game. Each aspect has been clearly illustrated by more than one hundred photographs and line drawings. As a bowler and a teacher, Norman Showers presents the student with the opportunity to learn and enjoy this popular game of bowling.

The tear-out student/teacher evaluation forms included in this revised book should be a real asset to both the teacher and the student.

Contents

History

A form of bowling played by Egyptian children around 5,000 B.C. resembled the game of bowling as we know it today. The early Egyptians used smaller balls or round rocks and egg-shaped pins.

Bocci, similar to present Italian bowling, was played in what now is northern Italy in about 50 B.C. The early Polynesians had a game which resembled bowling that used small balls and flat disc-shaped stones. The Polynesians rolled their bowling balls a distance of 60'.

The game of bowling became so popular in England around A.D. 1100 that it was outlawed by the king. The reason: men were spending too much time bowling and not enough time practicing archery, which was used for national defense.

Kegling was used by religious leaders during the middle ages in Germany to determine whether a person was living a good life. The priest would have a man set up his *kegel* (pin) and attempt to knock it down. If successful, he was assumed to be living an honorable life. Martin Luther was a bowling enthusiast in the early 1500s and is credited with standardizing the number of pins or *kegels* at nine. He also set the rules for the game of *nine pins*.

Bowling entered the picture again in England during the late 1500s. Sir Francis Drake was enjoying a game of *bowling-on-the-green* when informed that the Spanish Armada was approaching the English coast. Sir Francis sent the courier back with a message that he would not leave until the game was finished. It was not recorded whether he bowled so badly that he was mad and proceeded to defeat the Spanish, or that he bowled so well and was so elated that he engineered the destruction of the Armada. In either case one might surmise that bowling had some emotional effect upon the leader.

The Dutch brought the game *skittles* with them to New Amsterdam in the early 1600s. In Washington Irving's novel, *Rip Van Winkle*, mention is made of the thunder of balls hitting pins bowled by little Dutch men.

During the middle 1800s, *nine pins* were extremely popular in the New England states, especially New York, where alleys were found on almost every block. The popularity spread in such a manner that gambling interests took over. This caused the state legislatures in New York, Connecticut, and Massachusetts to outlaw the game of nine pins. It is not known who added the tenth pin and placed the pins in triangular formation. At times when the so-called ten-pin tap occurs, we would appreciate having only nine pins.

With the advent of *ten pins*, along with the extreme variances in the weights and sizes of balls and pins, as well as lengths and widths of bowling lanes, the *American Bowling Congress* (ABC) was founded in 1895 to promote and elevate the game. Several other attempts had failed to organize and supervise bowling properly, such as the National Bowling

Figure 1.1 Nine pin bowling set-up.

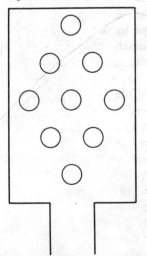

League in 1875 and the American Amateur Bowling Union in 1890. The ABC continues to set standards involving all aspects of the game. The *Women's International Bowling Congress* (WIBC) was organized in 1916 in St. Louis, Missouri, as the women's governing body. An organization for boys and girls was formed in 1941 and named the *American Junior Bowling Congress* (AJBC).

Bowling has evolved from something of a curiosity game to one of highly developed skill and huge bowling establishments. Bowling has emerged from the ill repute of early days, to a sport for family enjoyment, with some establishments offering baby sitting services.

The ABC, WIBC, and AJBC hold yearly bowling championships. The ABC and WIBC host the largest organized sports championship in the world. In excess of 5,700 men's teams usually participate in the annual ABC tournament. Over 6 million men and 3 million women, and 1 million college students and junior boys and girls are members of bowling leagues around the world, with most of the bowlers in the United States. Estimates have indicated that in the United States there are more than 40 million men, women, boys, and girls participating in some phase of bowling, with millions more around the world, and the number is increasing each year. Bowling is considered the largest participant sport.

Figure 1.2 Southern Illinois University lanes, Edwardsville, Illinois.

Terminology

2

Bowling has many interesting words and terms unique to *keglers*. If a bowler has *struck out*, for instance, there are those who might think this was bad; just the opposite, it is excellent, and getting a *foul* does not permit you to try again without penalty, as in baseball. The more common bowling terms are listed below. This is by no means a complete list. Many areas of the country have special terms which are unique to their own locality.

ABC American Bowling Congress (men's organization).

AJBC American Junior Bowling Congress (boys' and girls' organization).

ALL-EVENTS Total pins for nine games in a tournament composed of three games each in the team, doubles, and singles events.

ALLEY (see LANE).

ANCHORMAN Last bowler on a team. Usually the best bowler. (See Ch. 7, p. 89.)

APPROACH The area behind the *foul line*—at least 15' long—in which the bowler makes his approach.

ARROWS A series of seven triangular darts (spots) placed in front of the foul line. Spot bowlers use the arrows as aiming points rather than looking at pins when they release the ball (see Spot Bowler). See Figs. 4.16, 4.17, 4.18, 4.19, 4.24, 4.25, 4.26.

BABY SPLIT   The 3−10 or 2−7 split. (See Figs. 4.36, 4.42.)

BACKUP BALL   A ball that curves to the right for a right-handed bowler and curves to the left for a left-handed bowler. (See Figs. 4.18, 4.19, 4.22.)

BEDPOSTS   The 4−6 or 7−10 splits (see RAILROAD). (See Figs. 4.50, 4.52.)

BLIND   Score given for a missing bowler. Usually the score is based on 90 percent of the missing player's average.

BLOW   Failure to get a strike or a spare in a frame (see ERROR, MISS, or OPEN). (See Fig. 2.3 and Ch. 3, p. 15.)

BONUS   The number of additional pins scored when getting a *strike* or a *spare* (see STRIKE and SPARE). (See Ch. 3, p. 17.)

BREAK   Getting a lucky hit. Pins falling seemingly without any skill on the bowler's part. Failure to make a strike after getting several strikes in a row.

BROOKLYN   A right-handed bowler hitting to the left of the head pin or a left-handed bowler hitting to the right of the head pin, also called CROSSOVER. (See Figs. 4.33, 4.47.)

BUCKET   The 2−4−5−8 or 3−5−6−9 pin leaves. (See Figs. 4.34, 4.40, 4.48.)

CARRY   To knock down a pin or pins.

CHANNEL   A shallow trough about 9″ across extending from the foul line to the end of the *lane* also called GUTTER.

CHANNEL BALL   A ball rolled in the *channel*, also called GUTTER BALL.

CHERRY   Knocking down at least the front pin or pins during a spare attempt and heaving adjacent or rear pins.

CHOKE   Failure to accomplish the desired objective due to increased tension or anxiety.

CHOP   (See CHERRY).

CLOTHES LINE   The 1−2−4−7 or 1−3−6−10 pin leaves.

CONVERT   Ability to make a spare or split.

COUNT   Failure to get the maximum number of pins either with the first ball or second ball. (See Ch. 7, p. 92; Ch. 3, p. 15.)

CREEPER A slowly rolled ball.

CROSSOVER (See BROOKLYN.)

CURVE A ball which is rolled toward the outside of the lane and then curves back toward the center of the lane. There is a difference between a *curve* and a *hook* ball. (See Figs. 4.18, 4.19, 4.21, 4.26).

DEAD BALL A ball delivered on the wrong lane or out of turn. Also meaning that the ball has little or no spin, or does not knock down the pins that it seems should fall, also called *dead apple, flat apple,* or *sour apple.*

DEAD MARK Making a *strike* or a *spare* on the last ball in the tenth frame. No *bonus* allowed on a dead mark. (See Ch. 3, p. 15; Fig. 3.1; Ch. 7, pp. 92-93.)

DELIVERY Rolling of the ball. Also used to designate either the *curve* *hook, backup,* or *curve* ball delivery.

DOUBLE Two consecutive strikes. (See Fig. 2.1.)

DOUBLE PINOCHLE The 4–7–6–10 split.

DOUBLES Two players forming a doubles team.

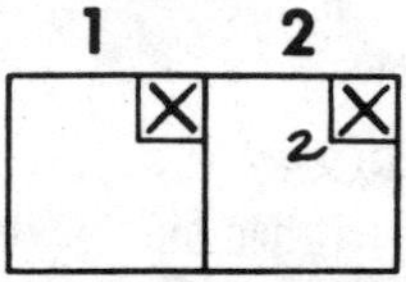

Figure 2.1   Double strike.

DRINK FRAME Usually the fifth frame of a game. The player knocking down the fewest pins on the first ball is supposed to buy the drinks for the team members. Also occurs if all team members but one get a strike in a frame; or in case all team members get a strike in a frame, the team captain buys the drinks.

DUTCHMAN OR DUTCH 200 Scoring a 200 game by alternating strikes and spares throughout a game. (See Fig. 2.2.)

ERROR Failure to *convert* a spare (not a *split*), also called BLOW, MISS, or OPEN. (See Fig. 2.3.)

FAST LANES Term given to slick lanes. Ball does not curve or track properly.

FILL BALL Last ball strike in the tenth frame. (See Fig. 2.8.)

FOUL Touching or going over the foul line when making a legal delivery. It is foul if you touch the wall, floor, or support beyond the foul line even if this occurs on another lane. It is *not* a foul if the ball is not released. A person who *deliberately* fouls to gain an advantage may be disqualified from the game, match, or remainder of the season. A foul is scored as if the ball was rolled into the channel (gutter)—no pin count allowed for that ball.

FOUL LINE A black line 60' from the center of the head pin which separates the approach from the lane. (See Figs. 4.12, 4.19.)

FRAME A player's turn during a game. A game consists of ten frames. (See Fig. 2.4.)

Figure 2.2 Dutch 200 game.

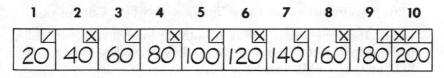

Figure 2.3 Error, miss, or blow.

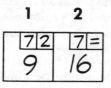

Figure 2.4 Frame of a bowling game.

GROOVE Lanes which may have a defect—a very shallow depression. High scoring lanes are often said to be grooved. Very, very few lanes have a groove.

GUTTER (See CHANNEL.)

GUTTER BALL (See CHANNEL BALL.)

HANDICAP A score adjustment based on the difference between the league averages of individuals or teams. The usual handicap is based on 75 percent of the difference between the averages, and this handicap is added to the score of the individual or team with the lowest average.

HEAD PIN The No. 1 pin.

HIGH BOARD Often on newly installed lanes a board will not fit exactly right, causing the board to be higher than the other boards.

HIGH HIT Usually associated with a ball that hits the head pin or pocket too full or even head-on.

HOLDING LANE A lane that keeps the ball from hooking or curving sufficiently.

HOOK A ball delivered in such a manner that it goes straight and then curves sharply to the center of the lane. A hook is often confused with a *curve ball* delivery. (See Figs. 4.18, 4.19, 4.20, 4.26.)

KEGLER Another name for a bowler. The early Germanic men were called keglers because they carried a *kegel* (pin) with them as protection.

KICK BACK Special boards placed on the restraining wall separating two lanes. Pins often rebound off the boards.

KING PIN The name given to the No. 5 pin. (See Figs. 4.30, 4.45.)

LANE The name usually associated with the wooden surface extending from the foul line to the end of the pin deck, also called ALLEY, LANE BED, or ALLEY BED. (See Fig. 3.4.)

LEAD OFF The first bowler on a team. (See Ch. 7, p. 89.)

LEAGUES Composition of a league may vary from as few as 3 or 4 teams to as many as 40 teams. Usually a league is composed of 8 to 24 teams. Leagues are designated as *handicap, scratch,* or *mixed* (men and women) leagues. (See Ch. 7.)

LEAVE Term given for the pins remaining after the ball has been rolled.

LIGHT HIT Occurs when the ball does not hit a pin correctly, causing considerable pin deflection, or when the ball does not hit a pin solidly enough, also called MIXER and THIN HIT.

LINE An individual's game of ten frames. Also refers to the path of the ball by some bowlers, also called *game.* (See Ch. 3, p. 19.)

LOFTING Releasing the ball late, causing the ball to sail through the air in an arc higher than normal. This often damages the lane surface. Caused when the ball sticks to a bowler's fingers, or done deliberately. (See Fig. 5.5.)

MARK A *strike* or *spare.* (See Fig. 2.5.) A mark is counted for each strike or spare (except no mark counted for last ball strike or spare in tenth frame—see illustrated game on scoring, p. 19) plus an additional mark for each consecutive strike with the exception of the second strike in tenth frame, which is counted as one mark. A mark is lost if a bowler fails to knock over at least 5 pins on the first ball following a spare or multiple strike.   A mark is lost if fewer than 5 pins are knocked down with both balls in a frame or following a strike.   Keeping track of the marks for each team during a game is one way to determine which team is ahead, as each mark counts roughly 10 pins; that is, if one team has 26 marks and another team has 21 marks, there usually is a difference of about 50 pins between the teams.   A mark is considered *live* during a game except if a spare or strike occurs on the last ball of a game.   (See Figs. 7.1, 7.2.)

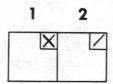

Figure 2.5   Mark (strike or spare).

MISS   Failure to convert a spare leave except on a split, also called a BLOW, ERROR, or OPEN.   (See Ch. 3, p. 15.)

MIXER   A ball which causes the pins to mix and spin in such a manner that other pins are knocked over, also called a LIGHT HIT, or THIN HIT.

NOSE HIT   A ball hits full or square on the head pin, usually resulting in s aplit such as the 4−6 or 4−7−6−10, also called a HIGH HIT.

OPEN   Failure to get a strike or spare in a *frame,* also called a BLOW, ERROR, or MISS.   (See Ch. 3, p. 15.)

PERFECT GAME−300   Recording a legal strike in all ten frames, resulting in 12 consecutive strikes.   (See Fig. 2.6, also Ch. 9.)

Figure 2.6   Perfect game.

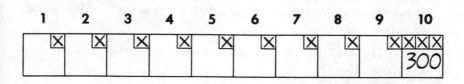

PIN   The regulation bowling pin is 15" high.   Most pins weigh between 3 pounds 2 ounces and 3 pounds 6 ounces.   The variance within a set of pins can be no more than 4 ounces.   Most pins are made of laminated wood with a thick plastic outer coating.

PIN BOWLER   A bowler who looks at the pins when delivering the ball. (Opposite of a SPOT BOWLER.)

PIN COUNT   Failure to get maximum pin fall either with first ball or with both balls in a frame. (See Ch. 3, p. 15; Ch. 7, p. 92.)

PIN DECK   The area on which the ten pins are spotted. (See PIN SPOTS.) (See Fig. 3.4, 8.7.)

PIN SPOTS   The spots on the pin deck on which the pins are spotted. The circular spots are placed 12" apart from center to center of adjacent spots. (See Figs. 3.4, 8.7.)

PIT   The area at the end of the pin deck into which the pins and the ball fall before being put onto the pin spotter and ball return. This area must be about 10" below the pin deck. The pit has a kick back (rear cushion) at the end on the wall or inside the automatic spotter.

POCKET   The 1–3 pins for a right-handed bowler or the 1–2 pins for a left-handed bowler. (See Figs. 4.18, 4.19.)

RAILROAD   Term associated with the 4–6 and 7–10 splits. Next to impossible to pick, also called BEDPOSTS. (See Figs. 4.50, 4.52.)

RETURN   Usually an under-the-lane track on which the ball is returned to the bowler from the pit.

RUNWAY   (See APPROACH.)

SANCTION FEE   Fee charged to each team or individual bowler by the local bowling association. A portion of the fee is forwarded to the ABC, WIBC, or AJBC to receive national sanctioning. (See Ch. 7, p. 90.)

SANDBAGGING   Name given to bowlers deliberately holding down their league averages to gain an advantage by receiving a higher handicap in league or tournament play. Bowlers may be suspended for life for this infraction. (See Ch. 7, p. 97.)

SCRATCH BOWLING   Bowling event in which no handicap is awarded to any player. (See Ch. 7, p. 91.)

SET-UP   All ten pins standing on the pin spots. (See Fig. 3.4.)

SINGLES   Bowlers competing by themselves.

SLEEPER   A pin leave combination in which one pin is directly behind another pin, such as the 2–8, 3–9, and 1–5 pins. (See Fig. 4.34.)

SLOW LANES   Lanes on which a ball curves or hooks easily.

SOUR APPLE SPLIT   The 5–7–10 pin leave combination. (See Fig. 2.7.)

Figure 2.7 5—7—10, sour apple split.

SPAN Distance between the thumb and finger holes. The 3 basic spans are a regular three-finger grip, semi-finger-tip grip, and the finger-tip grip. (See Fig. 4.1.)

SPARE Knocking down all pins in one frame with two balls. A bonus is awarded for making a spare. The spare bonus is the next ball rolled, except on a spare following a strike in the tenth frame. Scoring is 10 plus the bonus ball. (See Ch. 3, *Scoring.* There are 1023 possible spare combinations.)

SPLIT When an intermediate pin is missing in any series of pins, providing the head pin is not standing after delivering the first ball in a frame. In the tenth frame s plit may occur when delivering a bonus ball following a spare or either bonus fall following a strike when rolling at a full set of pins. Various splits include the following combinations: 4—5, 5—6, 7—8, 8—9, 9—10, 2—7, 3—10, 4—5—7, 5—6—10, 6—7, 4—10, 4—9, 6—8, 8—10, 7—9, 5—7, 5—10. (There are 459 possible split combinations.)

SPOT BOWLER A bowler who looks at the arrows or other aiming points rather than at the pins when releasing the ball. (Opposite of a PIN BOWLER.)

STEPS Refers to the number of steps a bowler takes when walking to the foul line to deliver the ball. Most players take either 4 or 5 steps to attain better scores. Better rhythm is gotten by using the 4 or 5 step approach. Bowlers who use the 3 step approach do most of their arm swing by forcefully pulling the arm through rather than by using a rhythmic arm pendulum swing. (See Figs. 4.11, 4.13.)

STRIKE Knocking down all ten pins with one ball, providing a foul or channel (gutter) ball did not occur. A bonus is allowed for a strike except after a second and;or a third strike in the tenth frame. The strike bonus allowed is the total pins knocked down with the next two succeeding balls except following the first strike in the tenth frame, in which case the two balls following a first tenth frame strike are bonus.

STRIKE OUT   Making three strikes in the tenth frame or finishing with any number of consecutive strikes in a game. (See Fig. 2.8.)

10

Figure 2.8 Striking out.

SWEEPER   A ball that seems to push the pins off the pin deck. (Often called a MIXER or WORKING BALL.) Also a singles tournament of 5 to 20 games.

TAP   Name given to an apparent good strike hit which leaves a pin standing. Good bowlers feel the only real tap is the 8 pin for right-handers and the 9 pin for left-handers, although the 7 and 10 pins are termed as taps.

THIN HIT   (See LIGHT HIT.)

TIMBER   Another name for a pin.

TURKEY   Three consecutive strikes in a game. (See STRIKE OUT.) (See Fig. 2.8.)

WASHOUT   Right-handers leaving the 1–2–10 pins standing after the first ball in a frame, or left-handers leaving the 1–3–7 pins standing. (Relates to a CLOTHES LINE.)   (See Figs. 4.31, 4.34, 4.48.)

WATER BALL   A ball delivered poorly, also called a dead ball or dead apple.

WIBC   Women's International Bowling Congress (women's governing organization in bowling).

WORKING BALL   A ball delivered in such a manner that the pins may spin and fly around getting pin action, also called MIXER, SWEEPER, or THIN HIT.

The Game of Bowling

PURPOSE

Bowling, in its simplest form, is a game in which a player attempts to knock down ten pins by rolling a ball some 60' on a smooth, level lane. From this brief description the game becomes increasingly complex.

A youngster may need to use a lightweight junior size ball and use both hands to roll the ball, another bowler may throw the ball with such speed that he literally knocks the back end out of the lane. Somewhere between is a more desirable speed at which to roll the ball.

The object of the game, then, is to roll a ball (maximum weight 16 pounds) at a set-up of ten pins (normally weighing between 3 pounds 2 ounces and 3 pounds 6 ounces per pin) and hopefully or skillfully knock down all ten pins with the first ball (for a strike) or with two balls (for a spare), and to accomplish these tasks while staying behind the foul line. A game consists of ten frames per bowler. Either one ball (strike) or two balls (spare) are rolled per frame, except in the tenth frame (last) in which a total of three balls are rolled if a spare or strike is made.

GOALS

All bowlers eventually have their sights set on a perfect game of 300. To score a 300 game, 12 consecutive legal strikes must be rolled in a single game. The chances of a man bowling a 300 game are rather slim, something like 1 chance in 366,000. The odds against a woman hitting a 300 game are as much as 10 times higher. An interesting sidelight is that there have usually been more holes-in-one in golf in a normal year than there have been perfect 300 games bowled in sanctioned competition since the ABC was organized in 1895. The first 300 game bowled in the annual ABC tournament was rolled by Billy Knox in 1913.

The goal of most men and women bowlers is to roll a 200 game. The hope of some keglers is to compile a league average of 200 or more. The bowling studies done by the author[1] on men bowlers and by his brother[2] on women bowlers revealed that male bowlers who attain a league average of 200 or higher and women who reach the 190 average level are in very select company, as only one in 1,000 bowlers reach this level of accomplishment. Other achievement levels relating to the league bowling averages are: approximately 5 in 1,000 men and women have averages in the 190's and 180's, respectively; 5 in 100 men and women average in the 180's and 170's, respectively; 15 in 100 men and women average in the 170's and 160's, respectively. The average league average was found to be 154 for men[3] and 126 for women.[4]

SCORING

To enjoy any game to its fullest you must know how to keep score. Bowling has a unique scoring system. In a game it is legally possible to knock down 10 pins per frame for the first nine frames and 30 pins in the tenth frame. This totals only 120 pins actually knocked over; however, the final score could be as low as 130, or as high as 300. Scoring may seem complicated at first, but once the fundamentals are learned, scoring is rather simple.

Basic Scoring Rules

1. *Miss* or *open* frame—score is the total pins knocked down with the two balls for that frame.

[1] Norman E. Showers, "A Study of Certain Factors Affecting Bowling Performance (Male)" (Master's thesis, University of Southern California, 1951), pp. 61–3.

[2] Robert G. Showers, "A Study of Certain Factors Affecting Bowling Performance of Female Bowlers" (Master's thesis, University of Southern California, 1953), pp. 68–70.

[3] Norman E. Showers, "Performance (Male)", p.70.

[4] Norman E. Showers, An informal study of 25,000 women's bowling averages in the St. Louis metropolitan areas, 1960.

2. *Spare*—score 10 plus a spare bonus of the pins knocked down with the next ball rolled, except on a spare following a tenth frame strike. Maximum score with a spare is 20 for a frame.

3. *Strike*—score 10 plus the strike bonus of the total pins knocked down with the next two balls rolled, except on the second and/or third strikes in the tenth frame. Maximum score in a frame with a strike is 30 pins.

4. *Be Accurate*—Make it a habit to put down the number of pins knocked down with each ball in a frame.

Scoring in bowling, as in other sports, has its own scoring symbols.

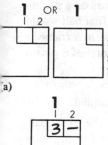

The frame (a) contains two small boxes; one box records the pinfall for each ball in the frame. Some score sheets have only one box. Note: there is a maximum of two balls per frame, except in the tenth frame.

This frame (b) shows 3 pins knocked down with the first ball A "—" denotes a miss, error, or blow with the second ball.

The frame (c) shows a total of 7 pins for the frame. Example shows 3 pins knocked over with the first ball, and 4 pins knocked over with the second.

The frame (d) shows 8 pins knocked over with the first ball, and a spare "/". The spare was made by knocking down the remaining 2 pins with a second ball. Score for this frame is not recorded until the player rolls the next ball, which would be the *first* ball rolled in the next frame.

This frame (e) shows all of the pins knocked down with the first ball for a strike "X". Score for this frame is not recorded until the *next two* balls are rolled in the following frame, or the following two frames if a second or third consecutive strike is made.

(f)

The frame (f) shows a split "O" left after rolling the first ball. The number of pins knocked down with the first ball is placed inside the split symbol. Two additional pins were knocked down with the second ball. Score for this frame is 8, and would be added to the total in the *previous* frame.

(g)

The frame (g) shows that a foul "f" occurred when delivering the first ball. No score is allowed on a foul for that ball rolled. When a foul occurs on the first ball, the pins must be respotted and a second ball rolled. Score for the frame is the total number of pins knocked over with the second ball—in this case 8 pins. (If a foul occurs on a second ball, only those pins knocked over with the first ball would count for that frame: If a player fouls twice in a frame, a *zero* score is recorded for that frame.) This total of 8 pins is added to the previous frame.

Now let us score a game, using the frames already examined.

Frame 1. (1) 3 pins were knocked down with the first ball. (2) 4 pins were knocked down with the second ball. (3) 7 is the *total* (3+4=7) for the first frame.

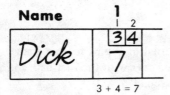

Frame 2. (1) 8 pins knocked down with the first ball. (2) *Spare* made by knocking down remaining 2 pins with the second ball. (3) No score is computed for the second frame until after the first ball is rolled in the next (third) frame.

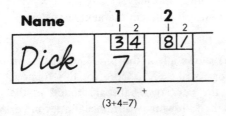

Frame 3. (1) *Strike* is made by knocking down all 10 pins with the first ball. (2) Now compute the score for the second frame. Add 10 plus bonus of 10 (first ball in third frame), which totals 20 (automatic 20 when a spare is followed by a strike or if a strike is followed by a spare). Total score in the second frame is 27 (7+20=27). (3) Score for the third frame must wait until the next two balls are rolled.

Frame 4. (1) *Split* occurs on the first ball. Only 6 pins were knocked down. (2) Additional 2 pins knocked down with second ball for a total of 8 pins (6+2=8) for the fourth frame. (3) Now compute the score for the third frame. Strike is 10 plus bonus of 8 (two balls in fourth frame), which is 18. Total score in the third frame is 45 (27+18=45). (4) Now compute total score for the fourth frame. Add 8 for the fourth frame to the third frame total of 45, making a total of 53 (45+8=53) in the fourth frame.

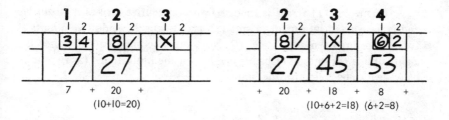

Frame 5. (1) *Foul* on the first ball. No score for this ball. (2) Pins respotted and 8 pins knocked down with second ball. Total pins for fifth frame is 8 (0+8=8). (3) Score in the fifth frame is 53 (fourth frame total) plus 8 (fifth frame score), which totals 61 (53+8=61).

Frame 6. (1) 9 pins knocked down with first ball. (2) *Spare* made by knocking down remaining pin with second ball. (3) No score is computed for the sixth frame until after the first ball in the seventh frame.

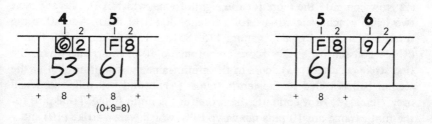

Frame 7. (1) 7 pins with the first ball. (2) Now compute the score for the sixth frame. Add 10 plus the bonus ball of 7 which totals 17. Total score in the sixth frame is 78 (61+17=78). (3) *Miss* occurs when no pins are knocked down with the second ball. Total pins for the seventh frame are 7 (7+0=7). (4) Compute the total score through the seventh frame. Add 7 for the seventh frame to sixth frame total of 78, making a total of 85 (78+7=85) in the seventh frame.

Frame 8. (1) *Strike* is made by knocking down all 10 pins with the first ball. (2) No score is computed for the eighth frame until after the next two balls are rolled.

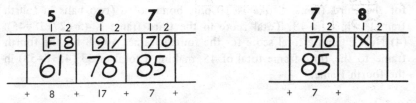

Frame 9. (1) *Strike* is made. Two consecutive strikes is a *double* and is designated by putting a small 2 next to the X. A double counts as two marks in the ninth frame. (2) No score is computed for either the eighth frame (as one more ball is needed) or the ninth frame (as two more balls need to be rolled for the bonus).

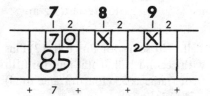

Frame 10. (1) *Strike* is made with the first ball. This makes three consecutive strikes, which is called a *turkey*. As was done for the strike in the ninth frame, a small 2 is placed at the bottom of the strike. Two more balls are rolled in the tenth frame if a strike is made on the first ball. (2) Now compute the score for the eighth frame, which is 10 plus the next two balls, which were strikes, for a total of 30 (10+10+10). Add 30 to the seventh frame total of 85, making 115 (85+30=115) in the eighth frame. (Three consecutive strikes score an automatic 30 in the frame where the first strike occurred.) (3) Score in the ninth frame must wait until after the second ball is rolled in the tenth frame. (4) Second ball rolled knocked over 7 pins. (5) Now compute the score for the ninth frame. Total pins for the ninth frame are 10 plus next two balls, which were a strike (10) and 7

for a frame total of 27 (10+10+7=27). Add 27 to the score in the eighth frame, which totals 142 (115+27=142) in the ninth frame. (6) A spare is made with the third ball in the tenth frame. (No additional bonus balls are allowed for this spare. We call this a *dead spare*.) (7) Now compute the score for the tenth frame. Add 20 (strike followed by a spare is an automatic 20) to the ninth frame score of 142, which totals 162 (142+20=162) as the final score of the game.

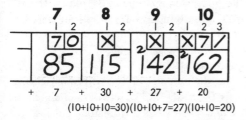

Notice the importance of making spares and strikes. There is an axiom that if you make spares the strikes will take care of themselves. Equally important is the necessity for concentration on *pin count* with every ball rolled. Never say, "Oh, well, wait until next frame." Always try to knock over every possible pin.

As can be shown in this game, if the bowler had merely made the maximum pin count each frame (even though not making a spare each open frame), this score would have been around 173 instead of 162. Many bowlers fail to realize that each pin left standing after the second ball on a strike is worth 2 points on the score sheet (we call this "pin count" or "get-the-count"). Sometimes certain pin leaves do not permit a player to get maximum count (9 pins), as in the case of a 4−7−6−10 split, in which case you should attempt to knock over the maximum pins available.

Bowling is more fun when you know how to score. Try your hand at figuring the hypothetical game shown. Also, how many good, live marks were made? The answers are at the end of this chapter. (See Ch. 7, Marks, pp. 92-95.)

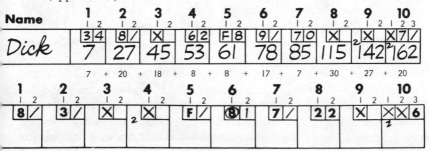

Figure 3.1 A hypothetical game: can you score it correctly?

EQUIPMENT

Bowling is one sport in which you may participate without purchasing any equipment. (See Fig. 3.3.) However, if you want to become good, you should have your own equipment. The bowling ball is the most expensive item, and in some instances you may buy a used ball at one of the bowling establishments for a modest price. Bowling establishments furnish house balls which may be used free. If you do not have your own bowling shoes, you may rent them for a nominal fee. If you purchase a bowling ball be sure you have a qualified person drill the ball to fit your hand. (See Fig. 3.2.) Fitting of the ball is covered in Chapter 4.

The bowling lane measures approximately 78' from the front edge of the approach to the back edge of the pin deck. The approach has a minimum length of 15'. The lane is from 41–42" wide with a channel on each side 4" deep and about 9" wide. The distance from the foul line to the center of the head pin is 60'. The pins are placed in a perfect triangle 36" on a side. The pins are 12" apart from center to center of adjacent pins. Bowling pins are 15" tall and made of laminated maple wood with a plastic outer coating and a plastic disc on the base. A bowling ball

Figure 3.2 Personal equipment and lane equipment.

Figure 3.3 Use proper equipment.

measures about 8½" in diameter and about 27" in circumference. The ball may not weigh more than 16 pounds. Most bowling establishments have automatic pinsetters. The pinsetter must be able to pick up those pins left standing and even pick up the pins that are moved off spot (even those that are wiggling), and then respot the pin(s) on the same spot from where they were picked up. If pins are touched and knocked over by the pinsetter, they must be respotted by hand on their original spot. Ask your bowling proprietor to let you observe these machines in action; most of them will be happy to show you around.

(Answer to the hypothetical game is 172. The number of good or live marks in the game is 7; four marks were lost—one each in frames one, four, seven and eight.)

Figure 3.4 Bowling lanes, pins, and pin spots.

Bowling
Fundamentals

4

Good bowling depends upon mastering the fundamentals. These include shoe and ball selection, stance, footwork, speed, type of delivery, and the sighting system. Although no completely perfect system exists, there are some well-established methods which have proven to be successful for many bowlers.

Every sport has certain fundamentals which tend to insure a participant the most success—bowling is no different. The emphasis in this chapter is on the most successful methods used to enhance maximum success and enjoyment. There are several styles and forms used in bowling; only those which have proven to be most successful are covered. The sequence used follows the most desirable order for individuals to pursue.

PROPER DRESS

Although it is not necessary to have a special uniform to bowl, you should dress comfortably with loose fitting clothes to allow freedom of movement. Tight fitting clothes hinder walking and sliding movements, as well as arm swing and follow-through. Members of teams usually have specially designed shirts or blouses which show the sponsor's name.

Shoe Selection. Bowling shoes are designed to allow you to start and stop properly. Although bowling establishments have rental shoes, it is in the best interests of the bowler to have his or her own bowling shoes. In the bowling studies done by the author[5] on men bowlers, and his brother[6] on women bowlers, it was found that those bowlers having their own shoes had an over-all league average about 5 pins higher than those not having their own shoes.

Bowling shoes are manufactured in many styles and colors to suit your taste. The importance of having your own shoes is that each shoe is designed for a specific purpose. (Rental shoes are for use by either right- or left-handed bowlers.) (See Fig. 3.2.)

Bowling shoes designed for right-handed bowlers have a soft leather sole and rubber heel on the left shoe (for sliding), and a rubber sole and heel with a leather tip on the right shoe (for starting). Bowling shoes designed for left-handed bowlers have a soft leather sole on the right shoe (for sliding), and a rubber sole on the left shoe (for starting), with both shoes having rubber heels. Bowling shoes are sized the same as regular footwear. There is a slight difference in the feel, as bowling shoes normally feel looser, allowing your foot to move slightly inside the shoes.

SELECTING A BALL

The bowling studies done by the Showers brothers[7,8] revealed that those bowlers owning a bowling ball had league averages about 10 pins higher than those who did not own a ball.

It is especially important that your bowling ball be properly fitted. Fitting of the ball includes a correct finger span, proper thumb and finger holes size, plus the weight of the ball. Bowling balls are manufactured in a variety of colors and weights. Personal preference will dictate the color you choose. You should select the heaviest weight ball that you can effectively control. Men should use a 16-pound ball unless physically unable. Many women are not strong enough to use a heavy ball, but the heavier the better. Robert Showers[9] found that women who used a 16-pound ball averaged about 5 pins higher than women who used a

[5]Norman E. Showers, "Performance (Male)", pp. 61–3.

[6]Robert G. Showers, "Female Bowlers", pp. 68–70.

[7]Norman E. Showers, "Performance (Male)", pp. 61–2

[8]Robert G. Showers, "Female Bowlers", pp. 68–9.

[9]Robert G. Showers, "Female Bowlers", pp. 45–6.

15-pound ball, about 12 pins higher than those who used a 14-pound ball, and about 26 pins higher than those who used a 13-pound or lighter ball. In general, bowling balls lighter than 12 pounds are for juniors.

If you use a "house" ball be sure you remember the serial number so you can find the same ball. All bowling balls have identification numbers on them. House balls usually have the weight of the ball stamped near the serial number. You may find that the ball you want is unavailable; usually it is not possible to go by the serial numbers in an attempt to find a ball with similar dimensions.

Fitting The Ball.   After determining the proper ball weight, the next step is to select a ball that fits your hand. If you buy a ball, have the ball drilled to fit your hand span. If your ball fits correctly you should not notice the weight of the ball as you deliver it. Another consideration in determining proper fit is whether you plan to use a *conventional, finger-tip,* or *semi-finger-tip* grip.   (See Fig. 4.1.)   Most bowlers use the conventional grip.   A guideline to follow in your grip selection is the control factor.   The conventional grip is easier to control.   Until you are consistently able to carry league averages higher than 180 it is not advisable to use the semi- or finger-tip grips.   Bowlers who have attained an average in the 180's have considerable control or accuracy and generally are able to master the special grips.   In all cases you should not have more than the thickness of a little finger between the ball and the palm when the ball is held at your side. (See Fig. 4.2.)

Conventional Grip.   In fitting for a conventional grip the first step is to place the thumb all the way in the thumb hole, making sure the hole is

(a)   (b)

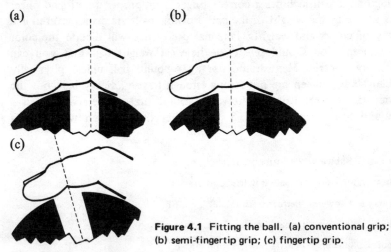

(c)

Figure 4.1   Fitting the ball.   (a) conventional grip; (b) semi-fingertip grip; (c) fingertip grip.

Figure 4.2 Holding the ball.

not too small or too large. The thumb hole should be slightly larger than your thumb. If the thumb hole is too large you will bend the thumb, which causes releasing problems—plus a sore thumb.

Next, with the thumb all the way in the thumb hole, spread your hand flat on the ball and extend the fingers as far as possible without over-stretching. Notice where the first joints of the middle and ring fingers are located in relation to the finger holes. If the bends of your first knuckle joints are approximately ¼" past the edge of the finger hole nearest the thumb hole, you have a correct span. A tolerance of ¼" either way is permissible. The finger holes should be a little looser than the thumb hole. If your span is too short, the ball will slip off your fingers when releasing, whereas if the span is too long, you may have trouble letting loose of the ball. In either case you may have some cramping in the fingers or forearm. (See Fig. 4.1.)

Semi-Finger-Tip Grip. *The fitting procedure for this grip is the same as that described for the conventional grip, with the following exception: The near edge (closest to the thumb hole) of the finger holes should be in the center* of the middle and ring fingers (halfway between the first two joints). The finger holes should fit snugly. This grip generates more digging power and is more difficult to control than a conventional grip. The semi-finger-tip grip is not recommended for bowlers with lower than a 180 league average. (See Fig. 4.1.)

Finger-Tip Grip. Follow the same procedure used in fitting for a conventional grip, except that the first joints of the middle and ring fingers should extend ¼" beyond the near edge of the finger holes. The main advantage of this grip is more digging power. It is considerably more difficult to control than the conventional grip, and produces slightly more curve and control difficulty than the semi-finger-tip grip. The finger holes should be tighter fitting than with the semi-finger-tip grip. This grip is not recommended for bowlers with lower than a 180 league average. (See Fig. 4.1.)

Ball and Shoes. Mention has been made of the advantage of owning a ball or shoes. There seems to be an additional advantage if you own both a ball and shoes. Bowling studies[10,11] revealed that those men and women who owned both a ball and shoes tended to average 22 to 32 pins better than those who did not own either a ball or shoes, 18 to 24 pins better than those who owned only shoes, and 7 to 23 pins better than those bowlers who had only their own ball.

PROPER STANCE

Now that you have a properly fitted ball and shoes, the next procedure is to assume a stance which allows freedom of movement while maintaining proper body balance. There are several styles which you may select; however, not all of them are conducive to good scoring. Only those stances which have proven to be most effective are discussed.

First, stand so that your body weight is evenly distributed on both feet. This may be accomplished by keeping both feet even or, if you are right-handed, by placing the left foot slightly ahead of the right foot, or, if left-handed, by placing your right foot slightly ahead of the left foot. Better balance is achieved if both feet are even, since there is a tendency to lean and/or turn your body if one foot is ahead. (See Fig. 4.3, 4.4.)

Second, hold your ball properly so that most of the weight of the ball is supported by the non-throwing hand. Very little weight should normally be supported with the throwing hand. The reason for this weight distribution is to allow you a more relaxed grip and better ball control on the pushaway.

Third, keep your wrist and forearm in a straight line. The wrist should be straight and firm, not rigid. Do not cup the ball or bend the wrist out. Notice the proper method of Fig. 4.6. Keeping the wrist firm

[10]Norman E. Showers, "Performance (Male)", pp. 61–2.

[11]Robert G. Showers, "Female Bowlers", pp. 68–9.

and straight permits a better pushaway and allows the ball to swing close to your body during the approach and delivery.

Fourth, hold the ball about waist high and next to your body as shown in Fig. 4.3. This method puts the least amount of exertion on your arms as well as maintaining better body balance. Some bowlers prefer to hold the ball chest high, which means the ball has to drop at least an additional foot, which many bowlers cannot effectively control. A ball held chest high does permit more speed during the delivery. The least effective method for most bowlers is bending forward with the ball, as this puts the body weight forward and, coupled with the ball weight, tends to cause body control problems in addition to follow-through problems during the delivery. In any case, whether the ball is held near the waist or above the waist, it should be close to your body. Holding the ball away from the body tends to cause you to lurch forward on the first step.

Figure 4.3 Starting stance, front view.

Figure 4.4 Starting stance, side view.

Figure 4.5 Proper methods of holding the ball.

Pushaway. After assuming a comfortable stance, swing the ball a few times to get the feel of it. Merely push the ball forward and out and then let the ball swing down in a pendulum motion (the action is similar to pitching a softball). Practice the pushaway and pendulum swing many times until they become second nature to you. Note: Do not attempt to force the arm swing.

If the stance and pushaway are not performed properly, the chances that you will be successful when releasing the ball are minimal. What you do at the beginning helps to influence your approach and body balance, and may cause the ball to be released incorrectly, which may result in poor balance at the foul line.

APPROACH

Now you are ready to *walk* (not run) to the foul line. The question is—how many steps should be taken? The number of steps you should take depends largely on preference. Many of the top bowlers estimate that footwork represents about 75 percent of your game (that is, footwork influences the other aspects of time, and so on). Therefore, you should determine the proper number of steps and proper starting position. One thing to remember as you take your steps: Keep your feet in contact with the floor (similar to a shuffle). Taking steps as in a normal walk may cause you to become off balance and wander as you approach the foul line.

Figure 4.6 Which way is best?

The usual number of steps taken by over 98 per cent[12,13] of male and female bowlers is 3, 4, or 5. Bowlers who use either the 4- or 5-step approach tend to have higher league averages by about 10 pins than do those who take 3 steps.[14,15]

The advantage in using either a 4- or 5-step approach is better rhythm during the approach, which results in a smoother pushaway and arm swing. The main disadvantage in using a 3-step approach is a decided tendency to overpower or throw the ball too hard, as well as a timing factor. A 3-stepper tends to walk as if walking over rough ground, which results in long strides. The 3-stepper is termed an arm-thrower because the ball is usually pulled through during the last step-slide. For these reasons it is advisable to use either the 4- or 5-step approach.

The 4-step approach is the more rhythmical of the two and is probably the most advantageous for the majority of bowlers. More advanced bowlers may find the 5-step approach to their liking as there are slight advantages over the 4-step, the main one being extra walking time, but this tends to increase some control problems.

Where to Start. To determine the proper distance from the foul line to start the 4-step approach: (1) Stand with your heels at the foul line and face the end of the approach, (2) take 4½ normal walking strides, (3) turn around (about face), and (4) you should be in the correct starting position. Women usually begin near the 12' dots and men about halfway between the 12' and 15' dots. (See Fig. 4.18.)

To determine the proper distance from the foul line to start the 5-step approach: (1) Stand with your heels at the foul line and face the end of the approach, (2) take 5½ normal walking steps, (3) turn around (about face), and (4) you should be in the correct starting position. Men usually begin near the 15' dots and women between the 12' and 15' dots.

The extra half step allows you enough room for sliding. It is important that you measure by using your normal walking strides, or you may end up by going over the foul line or stop too far away from the foul line. Ideally, you should stop about 2" to 6" from the foul line, and the closer the better. If you fail to start or end consistently in the same place, you will be off in your timing, ball placement, and speed of both the ball release and steps.

[12]Norman E. Showers, "Performance (Male)", pp. 36–8.

[13]Robert G. Showers, "Female Bowlers", pp. 36–8.

[14]Norman E. Showers, "Performance (Male)", pp. 36–8.

[15]Robert G. Showers, "Female Bowlers", pp. 32–3.

Figure 4.7 1st step, 4-step side. **Figure 4.8** 1st step, 4-step front. **Figure 4.9** 1st step, 5-step side **Figure 4.10** 1st step, 5-step front

The main difference between the 4-step and 5-step approaches is in the execution of the first step. As you begin the 4-step approach, push the ball away at the same time you move the right foot (right-handers start with right foot, left-handers start with left foot), just as though you had a string attached to both hand and foot as in Figs. 4.7 and 4.8.

In the 5-step approach move your left foot first (left-handers move right foot first), then move the ball forward as in Figs. 4.9 and 4.10. After the first step the 5-step approach is almost identical to the 4-step approach. In either case the first step should be short, just enough to get you moving.

Figure 4.11 4 step approach (front view).

As previously mentioned, the start of your approach is of utmost importance. Many bowlers fail to realize this and hurry; however, you should not walk too slowly either. What you do during the first step often determines whether you will: (1) walk too fast, (2) go over the foul line, (3) throw the ball too hard, (4) maintain proper body balance, (5) drop the ball at the foul line (let the ball go too soon), and (6) roll the ball over the desired spot.

During the first step the body momentum must go forward along with the pushaway sequence. If the first step is too long or too fast, lunging results and the pushaway will be too fast. If the first step is too slow the other sequences are usually too slow, with the result that you may speed up other phases. It is almost impossible for most bowlers to make adjustments after the first step. Although it is hard, you are better off if you stop (balk) and restart rather than continue a faulty approach (as happens when you sometimes brush your leg during the backswing).

4-Step Approach. Now let us analyze the 4-step approach from start to finish. Refer to Figures 4.11 and 4.13 as you read the description. Try the proper stance, pushaway, and approach without using a ball. You can try this at home; in fact, if you have a full length mirror, watch yourself do the various movements.

For the *First Step* assume your proper stance with body balanced and ball held about waist high. Simultaneously move your *right* foot (left-handers move your left foot) and push the ball forward and slightly downward (the ball continues forward and down through part of the second step). Note: Walk slowly, do not rush, and keep your eyes on

Figure 4.11 Continued

target. Body starts its downward tilt with normal walking motion. Keep your feet in contact with the floor, similar to a shuffle.

The *Second Step* begins automatically. You do not have to think through the movements consciously once the first step is started. The pushaway continues forward and down, beginning the pendulum swing. Your supporting hand should leave the ball automatically when you are about halfway through this step, with the ball and arm continuing the pendulum swing forward, down, and reaching the bottom of the swing just prior to starting the third step. Your body continues to become lower as you walk. Note: Keep eyes on target, walk slowly, do not rush, and let your arm swing freely; do not force the arm to swing. Keep your feet in contact with the floor. Keep your shoulders square to the foul line; do not drop your shoulder.

Figure 4.12 Picking up an object while balancing on sliding foot.

The *Third Step* should continue automatically; do not consciously think about taking this step. The pendulum swing should reach the highest point of the backswing at the conclusion of the third step, just prior to starting the fourth step. Note: Keep eyes on target, keep your shoulders square to the foul line, let your arm swing freely, and take your time; do not rush. Your body should continue its downward movement. Keep your feet in contact with the floor. Let the weight of the ball do the work. Do not force the arm swing. At the conclusion of the backswing, let your arm swing forward in a natural motion; do not force the ball.

The *Fourth Step* should continue automatically. At the beginning of the fourth step the arm swing starts its downward movement; do not force the arm forward. Note: Keep your eyes on target. As your fourth step is completed you begin the slide which is part of the last step sequence. The arm swings forward as you slide forward. The sliding foot should be pointing straight ahead in the same direction as your walk. Do not turn in your sliding foot, as this usually means that your approach is too fast, or that you may throw the ball too hard instead of rolling the ball, or both.

If you have completed your approach in good fashion, your sliding foot should stop about 2" to 4" from the foul line; the closer the better. The ball should be released a fraction after you stop the slide. The knee of the sliding leg should be bent. The bent knee movement is almost the same as if you were stepping forward to pick up an object on the floor. Stay balanced on your sliding leg. Your body should be square to the pins you are trying to pick. (See Fig. 4.12.)

RELEASE AND FOLLOW-THROUGH

Although the *release* and *follow-through* are treated separately from the approach, these movements are a continuation of the approach sequence. It is most effective if the ball is released 6" to 18" beyond (nearest the pins) the foul line. If the ball is released within this range you normally get more finger lift, and better ball control and follow-through. Body balance is better at the foul line if you have released the ball correctly, have proper timing, and a good follow-through.

On the follow-through, bring the arm up as if you want to shake hands. Do not let the arm swing across the body, as this results in pulling the ball. Reach for your target, keep eyes on target, do not look up from the target, and watch where the ball goes in relation to the target. The biggest mistake most bowlers make is not keeping their eyes fixed on their target when releasing the ball. After releasing the ball the middle and ring fingers of your throwing hand should be bent into the palm. You get almost the same release feeling if you lay a finger across the middle and ring fingers of your throwing hand and flip the finger off your release fingers. Note the three bowlers in Figure 4.14. The girl has released the ball too soon, the man in the middle has released the ball properly, and the man on the end has released the ball too late.

Notice the follow-through positions of the throwing hand and arm (Fig. 4.15). The girl has released the ball too soon and brought her arm directly across her body. The bowler in the center has released the ball properly, sliding foot straight, fingers in his palm, eyes on target, proper follow-through, and weight balanced on sliding foot. The bowler on the end is bent over too low, which does not allow proper finger release or follow-through (notice that the fingers are straight, with no real follow-through).

WHICH TARGET? SPOT OR PINS?

Which target should you use? There are two basic targets: (1) look at the *arrows* (triangular darts) beyond the foul line, or (2) look at the

Figure 4.13 4 step approach (side view).

bowling pins. Practically all better bowlers use the arrows (also called spots). Men and women spot bowlers tend to have league averages about 10 pins higher than those bowlers who look at the pins as they release the ball.[16],[17] The reason is that it is much easier to hit a close target than one which is over 60' feet away. A pin bowler must allow for the path of the ball even though he aims for the pins. The spot bowler needs only know the path of his ball, and then he can position himself so the ball rolls over the target spot (arrow).

The spot (arrow) which can be used most effectively by a majority of bowlers is the second arrow from the right side of the lane for right-handers and the second arrow from the left side of the lane for left-handed bowlers. (See Fig. 4.16.)

In conjunction with a spot (see Fig. 4.17), you must also stand in the proper place. Obviously you could not walk the same and roll the ball over the same spot each time and expect to knock down different pin leaves without moving either target or starting position.

It is simpler to look at a single target and merely change starting positions for each pin leave than to change targets as well as starting positions for each different pin leave combination. With this idea in mind, a discussion of the basic starting positions for strike and pin leave combinations follows the section on types of deliveries.

[16]Norman E. Showers, "Performance (Male)", pp. 28–30

[17]Robert G. Showers, "Female Bowlers", pp. 32–3.

Figure 4.13 continued

Figure 4.14 Which release is better?

TYPE OF DELIVERY TO USE

There are four basic deliveries: (1) *hook* ball, (2) *curve* ball, (3) *back-up* or reverse curve, and (4) *straight* ball. The method of releasing a ball determines whether the ball will curve, hook, back-up, or go straight. Left-handed bowlers seem to have a distinct advantage when delivering a ball, as they almost always roll a natural breaking hook or curve, whereas many right-handers have considerable difficulty learning to roll a hook or a curve ball.

Figure 4.15 Who has a better follow-through?

Figure 4.16 Target arrows for the right-handed and the left-handed bowlers.

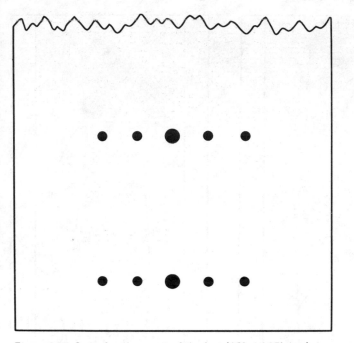

Figure 4.17 Spots for placement of the feet (12′ and 15′ dots).

The best scoring delivery for men and women was found to be a hook ball.[18],[19] Those bowlers who used the hook ball delivery averaged 5 to 10 pins better than the curve, 15 to 20 pins better than a back-up, and 20 to 25 pins better than those who used a straight ball. Figures 4.18 and 4.19 show the relative positions and paths of the deliveries.

Hook Ball. The hook ball (see Fig. 4.20) goes relatively straight down the lane before breaking sharply to the left for right-handers and to the right for the left-handers. This delivery has more digging action and pin action than the other types of deliveries. Except for the straight ball, the hook ball is the easiest to control. The release of the ball occurs with the thumb in the 11 o'clock position. The thumb comes out first, with the fingers following a split second later, which imparts an inward rotation to the ball as well as allowing the ball to roll forward. The ball actually skids

[18]Norman E. Showers, "Performance (Male)", pp. 40–2.

[19]Robert G. Showers, "Female Bowlers", pp. 32–4.

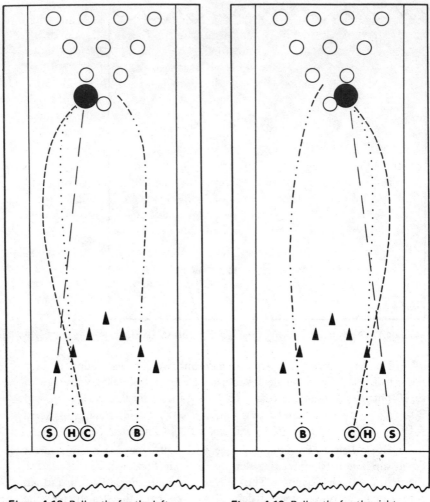

Figure 4.18 Ball paths for the left-handed bowler (B-back-up, C-curve, H-hook, S-straight).

Figure 4.19 Ball paths for the right-handed bowler (B-back-up, C-curve, H-hook, S-straight).

a portion of the way down the lane before the forward and sideward roll takes over. Let the finger lift and roll of the ball do the work for you. (Do not forcibly twist the wrist as this will impart a top spin, which is not conducive to good scoring and control for the majority of bowlers.) Maintain proper follow-through with the wrist straight and fingers in the palm.

Curve Ball. The curve ball (see Fig. 4.21) has a path that causes the ball to go out toward the edge of the lane and then curve back in a wide arc toward the center of the lane. The release for a curve ball occurs with the thumb near the 9 o'clock position. This delivery is usually more difficult to control than either the hook or straight ball, but is easier than the back-up ball. The main reason a true curve ball generally is somewhat lower scoring than a hook is the out-and-in path of the ball. The curve ball generates plenty of pin action but, since the ball moves so much, there often is not enough driving power for it to be quite as effective as the hook ball. The curve ball has considerably more scoring punch than either the straight or back-up ball deliveries.

The method of release, except for the thumb position, and follow-through are identical to the hook ball. The main difference between the two deliveries is that the curve must be directed out further toward the channel (gutter) to allow for the extra movement.

Backup Ball. This delivery is not recommended, even though there is a scoring advantage over a straight ball due to the curving action of the ball. The hand, arm, and body positions of the backup work against you, as can be seen in Figure 4.22. The majority of female bowlers throw a backup because of the physiological makeup of their wrist, elbow, and shoulder, which imparts a natural reverse twist at the time of releasing the

Figure 4.20 Hook ball release for the right- and left-handed bowlers.

ball. In order to throw a back-up it is necessary to twist the wrist to the outside in order to get a reverse twist on the ball.

Straight Ball. This is the lowest scoring delivery, as the ball rolls over the top in the same direction of the throw, which generally forces the pins straight back with little or no pin action. (See Fig. 4.23.) Players who use the straight ball delivery usually throw the ball harder, which adds to the complications and results in a lower score. Even though this delivery is easier to control, it is recommended that even a beginning bowler use either the hook or curve delivery because of their higher scoring potential (learn the best way from the start). The straight ball is released with the hand directly behind (under) the ball and the arm and hand swinging directly forward without turning or twisting the wrist. A straight ball has a tendency to fade away as the ball reaches the pins.

MORE SUCCESS FROM THE BEGINNING

Now that we have covered the basics of bowling, is there a better method for a beginner as well as for those who have been bowling a while? Yes, there is—if the methods which successful bowlers use are followed.

Theoretically, if you take 4 or 5 steps, spot bowl, and roll a hook or

Figure 4.21 Curve ball release for the right- and left-handed bowlers.

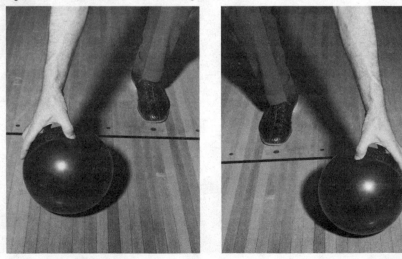

curve ball, your scores on the average should be about 40 pins higher than if you took only 3 steps, pin bowled and threw a straight ball. In addition, if you own a ball and bowling shoes, an additional 20 to 30 pins may be added, for a combined total of some 60 pins—so at least theoretically it is best to start on the right foot.

Remember, you must position yourself, hold the ball, look at a target, push the ball away, walk, release the ball, and follow-through properly to score well consistently. Many bowlers say they cannot think of so many things as they bowl—this is correct. All of the preliminary phases need not be conscious, as the first step is started only the target is watched; if the ball is released properly the follow-through will be all right. So in essence you must keep aware of approach speed, keep the hand in the proper position, keep your eyes on target, and then release the ball.

Knowing and doing the foregoing do not accomplish the trick of scoring unless you are able to get the ball to hit the desired pins and knock them down. The next phase of better scoring is to learn where to stand for the many varieties of pin leave combinations. Although each bowler may differ somewhat, the following discussion of starting positions for strikes and spares may be used as a guide.

Figure 4.22 Back-up ball release. (R.H.)   **Figure 4.23** Straight ball release. (R.H.)

STRIKES AND SPARES

Strikes

The desire of each bowler is to roll a perfect game. As previously mentioned, very few will ever attain this goal. The question is asked, "Which are more important, strikes or spares?" Naturally both are important to high scoring, but many bowlers become discouraged if they do not strike, and fail to concentrate on making the spare, which compounds the problem. A study of bowling scores by N. Showers and Gerber[20] showed that in all average categories men tended to average a fraction of a strike more per game than women. However, the women averaged a fraction of a spare per game more than men. To illustrate, men and women who had games between 160 and 169 averaged 3.09 and 2.71 strikes per game, respectively; however, they averaged 4.28 and 4.76 spares per game, respectively. In addition, the findings revealed that only those men and women who scored games of 200 or higher averaged more than 5 strikes per game. These statistics would indicate that strikes are important, but spares are the determining factor, since most bowlers will attempt to convert many more spares than strikes. Also, this tends to show the importance of pin count.

In an observation, done by the author at the 1971 ABC tournament held in Detroit, which involved 600 men bowlers participating in the team event, it was found that only 25 percent managed to get a strike on their first ball in their first game. In a follow up which included most of the same bowlers, only 30 percent were able to strike in the first frame the following day in the singles event.

Where to Start

Starting positions are determined by the type of delivery used, the amount your ball curves or hooks, and the pin or pins you want to knock down. The condition of the lane is also important. If you know how your ball reacts, then an adjustment may be made by moving your starting (foot) positions (this is covered in Chapter 6, "Finer Points of Bowling"). Line yourself up by using the 12' or 15' dots on the approach. Note: Do not guess; always make sure of your starting position. If you do not start at the dots, then line up directly behind the appropriate dot (use the same

---

[20]Norman E. Showers and Richard Gerber, "A Statistical Analysis of Men and Women League Bowling Scores". NCPEAM Proceedings. Chicago. 1969. p. 64.

board on which the dot is located). The main idea in converting various pin leaves is to use an *X* (see Figs. 4.24 and 4.25). That is, you stand on the side of the lane opposite from which the pin or pins stand; as the pins are left closer to the middle of the lane, you move nearer to the center of the lane.

Another item to fix in your mind's eye is that as you deliver the ball, the ball is released parallel to the line of approach while you are looking at the target spot, which is at an angle to your approach. Your sliding foot needs to point straight ahead toward the target pin as your arm swings straight ahead at the spot.

Now let us see where these various starting positions are located. Remember, *keep the same spot* for each throw. Move your starting positions rather than the spot for the various pin leaves. The following starting positions are projected for the average hook or curve ball. If you are right-handed place your right toe (center of the shoe) in line with the markings shown (see Fig. 4.26). If you are left-handed, place your left toe. (center of the shoe) in line with the markings shown. Do not worry about your other foot, merely bring it alongside of you in your normal standing position. Remember, you must start somewhere, so give yourself all of the advantage of a good starting position. Usually, if you are off target

Figure 4.24 Basic spare angles for left-handed bowlers.

Figure 4.25 Basic spare angles for right-handed bowlers.

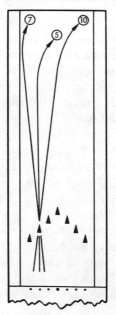

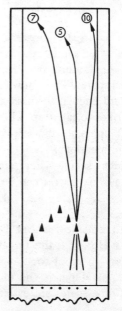

slightly, you will be close enough to hit the pins, which is much better than a hit-or-miss style.

Strike Positions. (1) Right-handers: Line up the center of your right shoe (toe) with the first dot to the right of the center dot. (2) Left-handers: Line up the center of your left shoe (toe) with the first dot to the left of the center dot. (3) Both: Stand with your shoulders square to the foul line. (Let your arm and ball hang down at your side. See Fig. 4.27.) Now bend both knees and let the ball down to touch the floor. The ball is directly in line with the outside dot. If you sight along a straight line to the *second arrow* from the channel, this is the path the ball should take if you keep your arm swing straight alongside your body as you walk to the foul line and roll the ball to the *second arrow*. Assume your starting stance. Walk straight ahead to the foul line, as shown in Figures 4.28 and 4.29. Try this several times from this position to be sure you are walking and releasing the ball correctly. There is a tendency to pull your arm across the body, which normally causes the ball to curve too much or to miss the spot. Be sure your arm finishes straight ahead and reaches for the *second arrow*. If your ball curves too much, move a couple of boards to the center of the lane and try again.

Above all, make sure you know where you are to start from; do not guess. Do not become discouraged if you do not make many strikes. Even the very best bowlers don't strike all the time. Try to roll a good ball that will leave an easier spare to convert.

Spare Positions. Spare shooting is the key to bowling. If you can consistently make your spares, the strikes will take care of themselves. More games and high scores are ruined because of open frames due primarily to missed spares. Some bowlers get disgusted if they fail to strike and do not try hard enough to make the spare on the premise that they will make more strikes to catch up. This is the wrong attitude.

Of the 1,023 possible spare leaves, there are about 150 relatively common spare combinations. No attempt is made here to show how to convert each different spare. There are seven basic positions from which almost all of the normal spares can be converted. Right-handed bowlers see Figures 4.30, 4.33, 4.35, 4.37, 4.39, 4.41, and 4.43. Left-handed bowlers see Figures 4.45, 4.47, 4.49, 4.51, 4.53, 4.54, and 4.55.

One point to remember is that the *key pin* in any combination is the pin closest to you. However, the target pin may or may not be standing. Often it is necessary to shoot for the pin that is not there; for example, in the 4–5 split the target pin is the missing 2 pin. Spares should not be considered easy. Some spares are easier to convert than others. Make sure

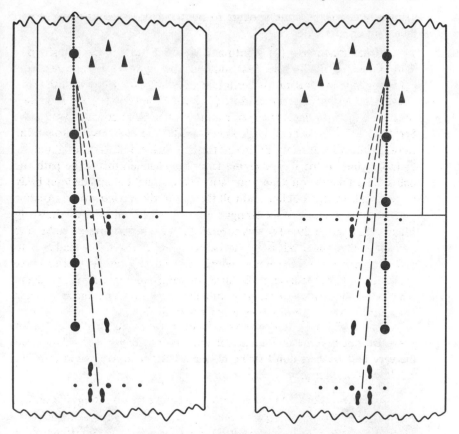

Figure 4.26 Basic spare angles for left-handed and right-handed bowlers.

Figure 4.27 Bend knees, let ball down alongside of you.

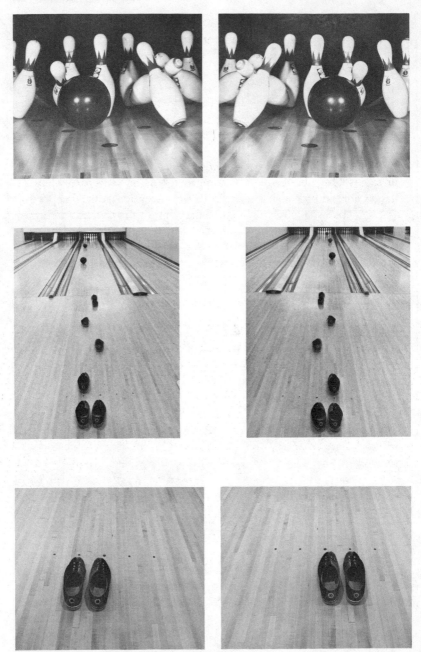

Figure 4.28 Left-handed strike sequence.   **Figure 4.29** Right-handed strike sequence.

you know what you plan to do before you roll the ball.

Right-handed bowlers have more trouble converting spares on the right side of the lane. Left-handed bowlers have more difficulty with spares on the left side of the lane. This occurs because of the curving action of the ball, which moves out or away from the pins and then curves back into the pins. Left side spares for right-handers and right side spares for left-handers are usually easier to make because the ball is curving into the pins rather than away. In general, use all of the lane width possible when shooting for spares.

Remember, *use the correct angles*, play the percentage shot, and your scores have a better chance to improve. You have approximately 22" of target area to pick a single pin, with the exception of the 7 or 10 pins. This distance is found by doubling the diameter of the ball, and adding the width of the pin. If you can keep a ball completely within the 22" target area (over half of the lane width), you should have no difficulty picking single pin spares. Another check is to notice the position of your sliding foot, as the foot should be pointing toward the target pin after releasing the ball.

Spare positions are discussed for both the right-and left-handed bowler. (Left-handed bowlers see pp. 54-64.)

Spare Positions for Right-Handers. In spare shooting, remember to use the maximum angle possible; that is, left side spares attempted from the right side of the lane, and right side spares attempted from the left side, and center spares from the middle of the lane.

Positioning of the feet is also important when you get into your starting position. Your feet need to be square to the foul line when shooting spares on the left side of the lane (pins to the left of center), and the starting position is on the right half of the lane. If the starting position is left of center, your body and feet need to be at an angle to the target spot. All spares discussed should be attempted by using the *second arrow from the right side*. Probable causes of leaving the various spares and their possible remedies are mentioned here, hopefully to produce more strikes.

5 Pin Spare (R.H.). Line up your right toe (center of the shoe) with the first dot right of center dot (same as strike position). Shoulders and feet square to foul line. Walk straight forward and roll the ball over the second arrow. (See Fig. 4.30.)

Some additional spares which may be attempted from this position include the following pin leaves: 1, 1–5, 1–3–7, 1–2–9, 1–2–3–5, 1–3–10, 1–3–6–7–10, 1–3, 1–3–6, 1–3–6–10, 5–8, 5–9, 5–8–9, 1–2–8–9, plus spares which include the 1–2–5 and 1–3–5 pins. *Usual*

Figure 4.30 Righthander's 5 pin sequence.

causes: (1) light or thin hit, (2) ball does not finish, (3) ball hits on Brooklyn side. *Usual remedy:* (1) concentrate on your hand release, more finger lift; (2) concentrate on your spot (arrow); (3) you may need to shift your starting position a couple of boards to right on thin hits, to left if hitting on Brooklyn side. (See Figs. 4.31 and 4.32.)

1–2 Pin Spare (R.H.) This is a Brooklyn hit spare. Line up your right toe halfway between the first and second dots right of center. Shoulders and feet parallel to foul line. Walk straight forward and roll the ball over the second arrow. Your sliding foot should be pointing toward the center dot at the foul line. (See Fig. 4.33.)

Other spares which may be attempted from this position: 2, 8, 1–2–4, 1–2–7, 1–2–4–7, 1–2–4–7–9, 1–2–8, 1–2–4–8, 1–2–10, 1–2–4–7–8, 1–2–4–10, 1–2–4–7–10, 2–7–8, 2–4–5, 2–4–5–8, 2–4–5–7–8, 2–5, 2–8, 2–4–8, 4–5, 4–5–7, 4–5–10, 5–10, 5–8–10. *Usual causes:* (1) missed arrow, (2) little or no finger lift, (3) rushing to the foul line, which causes body to turn and the ball to be released too soon, which in itself may cause 1 and/or 2 to happen. *Usual remedy:* (1) concentrate on your arrow; (2) get better follow-through; (3) walk slower. (See Fig. 4.34.)

4 Pin Spare (R.H.). Line up your right toe with the second dot right of center. Shoulders and feet square to foul line. Walk straight forward and roll the ball over the second arrow. Your left foot should be slanted toward the center dot at the foul line and also pointed toward the 4 pin. Your body will also be at a slight slant to the foul line. (See Fig. 4.35.)

Other spares which may be attempted from this position: 4–7, 4–8, 4–7–8, 2–4, 2–4–7, 2–7, 2–7–9, 2–4–7–10, 2–10, 2–7–10, 2–4–10, 2–4–7–9, 2–9, 2–4–9, 2–8–10, 2–5–7, 2–4–5–7, plus splits that are next to impossible to pick (go for maximum pin count), such as 4–6, 4–6–7, 4–6–7–10, 7–8–10. *Usual causes*: (1) missed arrow, (2) hit head pin too full, (3) too much speed on the ball, (4) ball curves too much. *Usual remedy*: (1) move starting position two boards to the left; (2) slow your approach; (3) concentrate on your arrow; (4) reduce the amount of curve by changing hand position. (See Fig. 4.36.)

7 Pin Spare (R.H.). Line up your right toe with the sixth board to the right of the last dot on the right (as if there were one more dot; some lanes have another dot). Shoulders and feet parallel to the foul line. Walk forward and roll the ball over the second arrow. Your sliding foot should point toward the center dot at the foul line as well as toward the 7 pin. Your body should also be at an angle to the foul line. (See Fig. 4.37.)

Other spare shots from this position (this position seems to be best when attempting to pick the following splits, either to pick the spare or get maximum pin count): 4–7–10, 4–7–9–10, 4–10, 4–9, 4–7–9, 4–7–8–10, 7–10, also 4–7. *Usual causes*: (1) high or light hit, (2) too much ball speed, (3) too much finger lift, (4) tough luck. *Usual remedy*:

Figure 4.31 1–3–7 spare (R.H.).

Figure 4.32 1–2–8–9 spare (R.H.).

Figure 4.33 Righthander's 1—2 pin sequence.

(1) concentrate on your arrow; (2) slow the ball; (3) do not exaggerate ball release; (4) better luck next time. (See Fig. 4.38.)

3 Pin Spare (R.H.). Line up your right toe just to the left of the center dot. Turn your feet and body slightly to the right. Walk at a slight angle toward your target and roll the ball over the second arrow. Your ball should track over the arrow, swing out toward the edge a little, and then curve back into the pin. Your sliding foot should be pointed toward the center dot and your body angled slightly towards the 3 pin. (See Fig. 4.39.)

Other spare shots from this position: 1–3, 1–3–9, 3–9, 1–3–8–9, 1–3–6–10, 1–3–6, 1–3–10, 1–3–7, 1–3–6–7, 1–3–6–7–10, 3–9–10, 3–5, 3–5–6, 3–5–6–9, 3–5–9, 3–5–10, 3–6–9, 5–6, 5–9, 5–6–10, 5–6–7, 5–7, 5–7–9. *Usual causes:* (1) head pin hit too full on left side, (2) missed arrow, (3) pulled ball across body, (4) approach too fast, which may cause your body to turn which causes you to miss your arrow, and may cause you to pull the ball. Usual remedy: (1) if you are rolling the ball

Figure 4.34

1–2–10 spare (R.H.).

1–2–8 spare (R.H.)

1–2–8–10 spare (R.H.)

2–4–5–8 spare (R.H.)

4–5 splits (R.H.)

4–5–7 splits (R.H.)

5–10 splits (R.H.)

2—4—7 spare (R.H.)

4—7 spare (R.H.)

2—7 baby split (R.H.)

Figure 4.35 Righthander's 4 pin sequence.

4—6 split (R.H.)

Figure 4.36

over the arrow, move your starting position about two boards to the left and use same arrow; (2) concentrate on second arrow; (3) follow through more; (4) slow down your approach. (See Fig. 4.40.)

6 Pin Spare (R.H.). Line up your right toe with the first dot left of the center dot. Turn your body and feet slightly more than for 3 pin. Walk at an angle and roll the ball over the second arrow. The ball should track over the arrow, swing out, and then curve back into the pin. Your sliding foot should point toward the center dot at the foul line, with your body facing the 6 pin. (See Fig. 4.41.)

Other spare shots from this position: 6–10, 6–9, 6–9–10, 3–10, 3–7–10, 3–7, 3–6–7–10, 3–6–10, 3–5–10, 3–6–7, 3–6, 9–10, plus splits that are next to impossible to pick (get the maximum pin count), such as 4–6–10, 7–9–10, 4–6–9–10. *Usual causes:* (1) hit head pin too full, (2) missed arrow, (3) ball curved too much, (4) pulled arm across your body. *Usual remedy:* (1) change your starting position two boards to the left; (2) concentrate on second arrow; (3) reduce the curve and/or move starting

Figure 4.37 Righthander's 7 pin sequence.

Figure 4.38 4—7—9 spare (R.H.).

position as mentioned; (4) walk slower and/or swing arm straight ahead and follow through. (See Fig. 4.42.)

10 Pin Spare (R.H.). Line up your right toe with the second dot (outside) to the left of center. Turn your feet and body so they are facing at an extreme angle (as if you were facing the 10 pin three lanes away). Walk at an angle to the foul line and roll the ball over the second arrow. Make sure you follow through. Follow-through is most important in picking the 10 pin; there is little room for error. Your ball should track out to the second arrow and then curve back down the edge of the lane. This pin is one which many bowlers have trouble picking due to a lack of confidence in themselves. Following the plan outlined should give you a better chance. (See Fig. 4.43.)

Other spare shots from this position (best when attempting to pick the following splits; get the count): 6—7—10, 6—7—9—10, 6—7, 6—8—10, 6—8, 4—6, 4—6—10, 4—6—7—10, 4—6—7, 4—6—9—10, 6—7—8—10. *Usual causes*: (1) too much speed on the ball, (2) too much curve, (3) too much finger lift, (4) too little finger lift, (5) bad break. *Usual remedy*: (1) slow down the ball speed by either walking slower, shorter first step, and/or slow arm speed; (2) reduce your curve and/or move starting position one board to the left if too much curve; (3) more finger lift by better follow-through and/or move starting position one board to right if not enough curve—concentrate on the release; (4) better luck next time. (See Fig. 4.44.)

Spare Positions for Left-Handers. The basic idea for you left-handed bowlers is the same as mentioned for right-handed bowlers.

3—5—6—9 spare (R.H.)

5—7 split (R.H.)

5—6 split (R.H.)

Figure 4.39 Righthander's 3 pin sequence.

Figure 4.40

Figure 4.41 Righthander's 6 pin sequence.

6—10 spare (R.H.)

3—6—10 spare (R.H.)

3—10 baby split (R.H.)

Figure 4.42

Figure 4.43 Righthander's 10 pin sequence.

That is, use the maximum angle available. Left side spares should be attempted from the right side of the lane, right side spares from the left side of the lane, and middle lane spares from the middle of the lane.

The placement of the feet at your starting position is important. If the starting position is to the left of center, both body and feet should be parallel to the foul line, with your feet pointing straight ahead. If your starting position is to the right of center, your body and feet need to be at an angle to the foul line.

All spares discussed should be attempted by using the *second arrow* (spot) from the *left side* of the lane. Probable causes of leaving the various spares and their possible remedies are mentioned here, hopefully to produce more strikes.

5 Pin Spare (L.H.). Line up your left toe (center of the shoe) with first dot left of center dot (same as strike position). Shoulders and feet square to foul line. Walk straight forward and roll the ball over the second arrow. (See Fig. 4.45.)

Some additional spares which may be attempted from this position include the following pin leaves: 1, 1–5, 1–2–10, 1–3–8, 1–2–3–5,

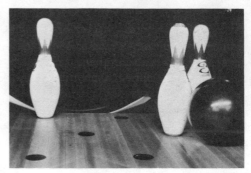

Figure 4.44 6—8—10 split (R.H.)

1–2–7, 1–2–4–7–10, 1–2, 1–2–4, 1–2–4–10, 5–8, 5–9, 5–8–9, 1–3–8–9, plus spares which involve the 1–2–5 and 1–3–5 pins. *Usual causes*: (1) light or thin hit, (2) ball fails to finish, (3) ball hits 1–3 (Brooklyn) pins. *Usual remedy*: (1) concentrate on your hand release—more finger lift; (2) concentrate on your spot (arrow); (3) you may need to shift your starting position a couple of boards to the left on thin hits—to right if hitting Brooklyn side. (See Fig. 4.46.)

    1–3 Pin Spare (L.H.). This is the Brooklyn side spare. Line up your left toe halfway between the first and second dots left of center. Shoulders and feet parallel to foul line. Walk straight forward and roll the ball over the second arrow. Your sliding foot should be pointing toward the center dot at foul line. (See Fig. 4.47.)

    Other spares which may be attempted from this position: 3, 9, 1–3–6, 1–3–10, 1–3–6–10, 1–3–6–8–10, 1–3–9, 1–3–7–9, 1–3–6–9, 1–3–6–9–10, 1–3–7, 1–3–6–7, 1–3–6–7–10, 3–9–10, 3–5–6, 3–5–6–9, 3–5–6–9–10, 3–5, 3–9, 3–6–9, 5–6, 5–6–10, 5–6–7, 5–7, 5–7–9. *Usual causes*: (1) missed arrow, (2) little or no finger lift, (3) rushing to the foul line, which causes the body to turn and the ball to be released too soon, which in itself may cause 1 and/or 2 to happen. *Usual remedy*: (1) concentrate on second arrow; (2) get better follow-through; (3) walk slower. (See Fig. 4.48.)

    6 Pin Spare (L.H.). Line up your left toe with the second dot left of center. Shoulders and feet square to foul line. Walk straight forward and roll the ball over the second arrow. Your sliding foot should be pointed toward the center dot at the foul line and toward the 6 pin. Your body

Figure 4.45 Lefthander's 5 pin sequence.

should also be at a slight slant to the foul line. (See Fig. 4.49.)

Other spare shots from this position: 6–10, 6–9, 6–9–10, 3–6, 3–6–10, 3–10, 3–8–10, 3–7–10, 3–6–7–10, 3–7, 3–6–7, 3–6–7–10, 3–8, 3–6–8, 3–7–9, 3–5–10, 3–5–6–10, plus splits that are next to impossible to pick (get the maximum pin count), such as 4–6, 4–6–7, 4–6–7–10, 7–9–10. *Usual causes:* (1) missed arrow, (2) hit head pin too full, (3) too much ball speed, (4) ball curved too much. *Usual remedy:* (1) move starting position two boards to the right; (2) slow your approach; (3) concentrate on your arrow; (4) reduce the amount of curve by changing the hand position at release. (See Fig. 4.50.)

10 Pin Spare (L.H.). Line up your left toe with the sixth board to the left of the last dot on the left (as if there were one more dot; some lanes have another dot). Shoulders and feet parallel to the foul line. Walk forward and roll the ball over the second arrow. Your sliding foot should point toward the center dot at the foul line as well as toward the 10 pin. Your body should also be at an angle to the foul line. (See Fig. 4.51.)

Figure 4.46 1—3—8—9
spare (L.H.).

Other spare shots from this position (best when attempting to pick the following splits, either to pick the spare or get maximum pin count): 6—7—10, 6—7, 6—8, 6—7—9—10, 6—7—8—10, 7—10, also 6—10. *Usual causes*: (1) high or light hit, (2) too much ball speed, (3) too much finger lift, (4) tough luck. *Usual remedy*: (1) concentrate on your arrow; (2) roll the ball slower; (3) do not exaggerate ball release; (4) better luck next time. (See Fig. 4.52.)

2 Pin Spare (L.H.). Line up your left toe just to the right of the center dot. Turn your feet and body slightly to the left. Walk at a slight angle toward the target and roll the ball over the second arrow. Your ball should track over the arrow, swing out toward the edge a little, and then curve back into the pin. Your sliding foot should be pointed toward the center dot and your body angled slightly toward the 2 pin. (See Fig. 4.53.)

Other spare shots from this position: 1—2, 1—2—8, 2—8, 1—2—8—9, 1—2—4—7, 1—2—4, 1—2—7, 1—2—10, 1—2—4—10, 1—2—4—7—10, 2—8—7, 2—5, 2—4—5, 2—4—5—8, 2—5—8, 2—5—7, 2—4—8, 4—5, 4—5—7, 4—5—10, 5—10, 5—8, 5—8—10. *Usual causes*: (1) hit head pin too full on left side, (2) missed second arrow, (3) pulled ball across body, (4) approach too fast, which may cause your body to turn, which causes

1—3—7—9 spare (L.H.)

1—3—9 spare (L.H.)

3—5—6—9 spare (L.H.)

Figure 4.47 Lefthander's 1—3 pin sequence

Figure 4.48.

Figure 4.49 Lefthander's 6 pin sequence.

you to miss second arrow, and may cause you to pull the ball. *Usual remedy:* (1) if you are rolling the ball over second arrow, move your starting position about two boards to the right and use same arrow; (2) concentrate on second arrow; (3) follow through more; (4) slow your approach.

4 Pin Spare (L.H.). Line up your left toe with the first dot right of the center dot. Turn your body and feet slightly more than for the 2 pin. Walk at an angle and roll the ball over the second arrow. The ball should track over the arrow, swing out, and then curve back into the pin. Your sliding foot should point toward the center dot at the foul line, with your body facing the 4 pin. (See Fig. 4.54.)

Other spare shots from this position: 4–7, 4–8, 4–7–8, 2–7, 2–7–10, 2–10, 2–4–7–10, 2–4–7, 2–5–7, 2–4–10, 2–4, 7–8, plus splits that are next to impossible to make (get the count), such as 4–6–7, 7–8–10, 4–6–7–8. *Usual causes:* (1) hit head pin too full, (2) missed arrow, (3) ball curved too much, (4) pulled arm across body, (5) walked too fast. *Usual remedy:* (1) change your starting position two boards to the right;

Figure 4.50 4—6 split (L.H.).

(2) concentrate on second arrow; (3) reduce the curve and/or move starting position as mentioned; (4) walk slower and/or swing arm straight ahead and follow-through.

7 Pin Spare (L.H.). Line up your left toe with the second dot (outside) to the right of center. Turn your feet and body so they are facing at an extreme angle (as if you were facing the 7 pin three lanes away). Walk at an angle to the foul line and roll the ball over the second arrow. Make sure you follow through. Follow-through is most important in picking the 7 pin; there is little room for error. Your ball should track out to the second arrow and curve along the edge of the lane. This pin is one which many bowlers have trouble picking due to a lack of confidence in themselves. Following the plan outlined should give you a better chance. (See Fig. 4.55.)

Other spare shots from this position (best when attempting to pick the following splits; get the count): 4–7–10, 4–7–8–10, 4–10, 4–7–9, 4–9, 4–6, 4–6–7, 4–6–7–10, 4–6–10, 4–6–7–8, 4–7–9–10. *Usual causes*: (1) too much ball speed, (2) too much curve, (3) too much finger lift, (4) too little finger lift, (5) bad break. *Usual remedy*: (1) slow down the ball speed either by walking slower, using shorter first step, and/or slower arm speed; (2) reduce your curve and/or move starting position one board to the right if too much curve; (3) more finger-lift by better follow-through and/or move starting position one board to the left if not enough curve; concentrate on the release; (4) better luck next time.

Figure 4.51 Lefthander's 10 pin sequence.

Spare Combinations. Over 140 spare combinations have been covered for both the right- and left-handed bowler. You may wonder how many of these you might expect to encounter during a series of games. During a string of 27 league games, the author had 16 different split combinations. A survey of 50 students in two college bowling classes, who reported the number of different pin leave combinations which occurred after the first ball in each frame for ten games, revealed that on the average each student had 45 different spare combinations, including 6.5 different splits. Although these seem high, we do shoot at a large variety of pin leaves. The most reported by a student was 86, and 21 was the least. You might give this a try yourself: just tabulate what pins are left after the first ball is rolled in each frame, then count the combinations after a series of ten or more games. There are some rather strange pin leaves which occur; one is the 5–7–10 (sour apple split), (see Fig. 2.7), and at least two reports have verified the 7–8–9–10 (back row) split. (See Fig. 4.56.)

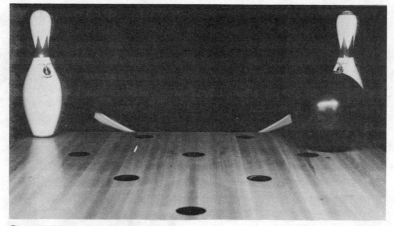

Figure 4.52 7—10 split (L.H.).

The importance of picking up your spares cannot be overemphasized. You should learn the most advantageous position from which to attempt to pick the various spares. *Play the percentages, pay attention to details, take your time, do not hurry.* Make sure you begin your approach from the correct starting position; do not indiscriminately change until you know what is happening. The best method is to get a qualified bowling instructor to watch you bowl. Practically all bowling establishments have trained and qualified instructors to help, if asked.

IS PRACTICE WORTHWHILE?

The adage that practice makes perfect may not be exactly true, but in bowling it surely does help the scores in the long run. The findings related to practice in the studies done by the Showers brothers[21,22] revealed that those bowlers who practiced three or more games per week had league averages 12½ pins higher for men and 9 pins higher for women than those bowlers who practiced one game or less per week.

Additional findings showed that the men and women who bowled in the greater number of leagues per week also had higher averages; that is, those bowling in two leagues averaged 15 to 17 pins higher than those who

[21] Norman E. Showers, "Performance (Male)", pp. 24—5.

[22] Robert G. Showers, "Female Bowlers", pp. 24—6.

Figure 4.53 Lefthander's 2 pin sequence.

Figure 4.54 Lefthander's 4 pin sequence.

bowled in one league, and men
and women who bowled in
four leagues had averages 25
to 29 pins higher than the
once-a-week bowlers.[23,24]
Similar results were noted
relative to the total number
of league games bowled during
the year.

These studies also showed
that the longer you bowl, the
higher you may expect your
bowling average to climb.
Both men and women who
had been bowling 16 or more
years had league averages 34
pins higher than those who
had been bowling a total of
three years or less.[25,26] This
trend was noted throughout
the range of years.

Not only does your average
tend to improve with practice
(of course there is usually a
leveling off), but there seems
to be a probability of scoring
higher single games and three-
game series. Those men and
women who reported a high
game between 200 and 220
averaged about 147 in league.
Women who scored higher
than 280 averaged 182 in

[23]Norman E. Showers, "Performance (Male)", pp. 20–2.

[24]Robert G. Showers, "Female
Bowlers", pp. 20–1.

[25]Norman E. Showers, "Performance (Male)", pp. 52–4.

[26]Robert G. Showers, "Female
Bowlers", pp. 59–61.

Figure 4.55 Lefthander's 7 pin
sequence.

Figure 4.56 7—8—9—10 split.

league, and men had a 189 average. In the three-game series category, bowlers who totalled between 600 and 649 averaged 170 for men and 164 for women. These averages rose to 180 for men and 178 for women with a series between 650 and 699, and for those who totalled 700 or better, both men and women averaged 195 in league.[27,28]

DIAGNOSTIC QUIZ

As one bowls, several questions arise relating to the various aspects of bowling.

1. Why select a heavy ball?
2. Why do bowling shoes have leather soles?
3. Why is it important that a ball fit your hand?
4. Does it make any difference how you hold the ball?
5. Which stance is most beneficial?
6. What is involved in the pushaway?
7. Why are the 4- or 5-step approaches better than the 3-step approach?
8. How do you determine your correct starting position?
9. How does the first step affect your timing, approach, and follow-through?
10. How should you release the ball? Where should the ball be released in relation to the foul line?

[27]Norman E. Showers, "Performance (Male)", pp. 56—60.

[28]Robert G. Showers, "Female Bowlers", pp. 64—9.

11. Why is spot (arrow) bowling better than pin bowling?
12. Which arrow is most advantageous to use?
13. Why not change your arrows for each different pin leave, rather change starting positions?
14. What advantages are there in rolling a hook or curve?
15. Which pin or pins are you most likely to leave on a full head pin hit? Light hit? Brooklyn hit?
16. Is practice worthwhile? Bowling in league?
17. If you are a right-handed bowler, what is the advantage of walking straight ahead when shooting for spares on the left half of the lane?
18. If your pins are on the right side of the lane, how should you face the pins?
19. Why does the 7-pin seem to be more difficult to pick for a left-handed bowler than for a right-handed bowler? Ten-pin for a right-hander?
20. Why is the proper fitting of the ball to your hand so important? how can you tell if the ball fits your hand?

Common Faults, Symptoms, and Remedies

5

There are several common faults which you may commit (without being aware of committing them) at one time or another. Most of these faults are correctable or can be minimized if you or an observer can diagnose the problem. A number of the more common faults, along with probable symptoms and remedies, are covered in alphabetical order. Not all symptoms and/or remedies will apply to all bowlers who have a common fault. In general, most poor shots are caused by the bowler taking his eyes off the arrow (looking up) when releasing the ball. Looking up may cause other faults, such as improper ball release, pulling, flipping, poor follow-through, and poor balance at the foul line. *Stay at the foul line until your ball hits the pins.*

The following list of common faults, symptoms, and remedies are not necessarily foolproof, but they should give you a guide to follow. When making adjustments based on the remedies, follow these instructions:

1. *Make sure you are committing the fault frequently or consistently* —doing something wrong intermittently happens to all bowlers, novice and expert alike.

2. After you have determined the basic problem (make sure it is the basic problem

and not a part of the basic problem), try one adjustment at a time, or possibly two if you are careful.

3. Be sure you continue doing the other phases exactly as you were except for the change (there is a tendency to do something else differently when a change is made—you get a different perspective).

4. Pay strict attention to your results. One of the worst faults a bowler can have is to keep making adjustments without a reason.

5. Check the basic spare positions in ch. 4 for additional information.

Figure 5.1 Poor backswing.

Figure 5.2 Maintain proper balance. Which one is properly balanced?

Figure 5.3 Sidewheeling.

Figure 5.4 Methods of holding the ball when starting

Figure 5.5 Don't loft the ball.

Common Faults	Symptoms	Possible Remedies
Backswing, poor (See Fig. 5.1)	1. Bent arm.	1. Straighten arm to allow pendulum swing.
	2. Too high.	2. Push ball away slower, hold ball lower, walk slower, or combinations of these.
	3. Too low.	3. Push ball away faster, hold ball higher, walk faster, or combinations of these.
Balance, poor (See Fig. 5.2)		
1. At starting position	1. (a) Lean forward.	1. (a) Hold body more erect, ball close to body.
	(b) Lean to side.	(b) Hold ball in center and close to body.
	(c) Weight mostly on one foot.	(c) Put equal weight on both feet.
2. During approach	2. (a) Wander, walk in zig-zag manner.	2. (a) Walk in a straight line, do not lean to either side.
	(b) Swing ball behind your back.	(b) Keep ball swinging directly alongside your body, do not turn body.
3. At the foul line	3. (a) Lean forward.	3. (a) Straighten up your back a little.
	(b) Body sideways.	(b) Walk in a straight line, slow down.
	(c) Sliding foot turned in.	(c) Walk slower, take shorter first step, don't try to roll the ball fast; see also (d).
	(d) Foot foul.	(d) Keep weight over sliding foot; see also (c).
	(e) Hop to side.	(e) See *hopping;* see also (c,d).
	(f) Placing hand on knee of sliding foot.	(f) Keep non-throwing hand out and away from the body, use as a counterbalance.
	(g) Sliding leg rigid.	(g) Bend sliding leg knee.
Ball release, poor		
1. Too much curve (See Figs. 4.20, 4.21.)	1. (a) Dives or misses pin.	1. (a) Change thumb release position closer to 11 o'clock, change starting position, or both. (See Fig. 4.14.)
	(b) Speed too slow.	(b) Speed up either pushaway, approach, or both.
	(c) Lane conditions.	(c) If cause is the lane, try (a) and/or (b).
	(d) Too much finger-lift.	(d) Do not exaggerate finger release.

Common Faults	Symptoms	Possible Remedies
2. Not enough curve (See Figs. 4.20, 4.21)	2. (a) Does not get up to desired pocket or pins.	2. (a) Change ball release to 9 o'clock, release ball beyond foul line, change starting position, or both.
	(b) Ball skids.	(b) Slow down, reach for target.
	(c) Flexing wrist.	(c) Keep wrist straight; see *flipping ball.*
	(d) Ball released wrong.	(d) Proper release between 9 and 11 o'clock
	(e) Hand under ball.	(e) Hold ball with hand in proper position.
	(f) Fingers straight as ball released.	(f) Flex fingers into palm at release, bend elbow on follow-through.
	(g) Missed arrow (spot).	(g) Watch arrow, roll ball over arrow.
3. Straight ball (See Fig. 4.23)	3. (a) Missed target.	3. (a) Change hand toward 9 o'clock position.
	(b) Fingers and arm straight.	(b) Flex fingers, bend elbow, follow-through.
	(c) Hand under ball.	(c) See (a).
4. Back-up or reverse curve (See Fig. 4.22)	4. Ball curves to right for right-handed bowler.	4. Release ball with thumb between 9 and 11 o'clock position, do not turn wrist out.
5. Ball does not finish	5. Ball deflects, does not keep digging.	5. Follow through more, flex fingers into palm; see (2) above.
6. Ball has too much speed	6. (a) Walk too fast.	6. (a) Walk slower, take your time, shorter first step; see (b).
	(b) Throw too hard.	(b) Slower pushaway, lower backswing; see (a).
7. Drop ball too soon	7.	7. See *dropping ball.*
8. Loft ball at release	8.	8. See *lofting ball.*
Brooklyn hit (See Figs. 4.33, 4.47)	1. Ball hits 1–2 pins (R.H.), 1–3 pins (L.H.)	1. and 2. Keep your head and eyes on arrow, walk straight.
	2. Ball hits to left (R.H.), to the right (L.H.),	
	3. Arm crosses the body.	3. See *pulling the ball;* see also (1) and (2) above.

Common Faults	Symptoms	Possible Remedies
Cupping the ball (See Fig. 4.6)	1. Wrist bent in. 2. Arm swings out.	1 and 2. Keep throwing hand and wrist straight; see *follow-through*.
	3. Sidewheeling.	3. See *sidewheeling*.
	4. Dropped shoulder.	4. Straighten body, reach forward.
	5. Turning the body.	5. See *foot turned*.
	6. Flipping the ball.	6. See *flipping the ball*.
	7. Lofting the ball.	7. See *lofting the ball*.
	8. Dropping the ball.	8. See *dropping the ball*.
Dropping the ball or bouncing	1. Released too soon. 2. Touches floor too soon.	1 and 2. Walk slower, keep body more erect, more backswing, roll the ball.
	3. Walking too fast.	3. Slow down, reduce arm swing speed.
Finger-lift, poor 1. Not enough (See Figs. 4.14, 4.15)	1. (a) Ball not finishing. (b) Ball too straight. (c) Leaves certain pins, like the 5, 5–7, 5–10.	1. (a,b,c) Follow through more, bend elbow, flex fingers into palm, walk slower; see *ball release* (2,3,5,6).
2. Too much	2. (a) Ball finishes strong. (b) Too much hook, curve. (c) Consistently leaves wide splits or 4, 6 pins.	2. (a,b,c) Speed up the ball, change starting position, less finger action, walk faster, swing arm straight; see *ball release* (1).
Flipping the ball	1. Ball skids too much. 2. Ball does not curve. 3. Some lofting of ball.	1,2, and 3. Keep wrist straight and firm, keep eyes on arrow, walk slower, do not try to put "stuff" on ball.

Common Faults		Symptoms		Possible Remedies
Follow-through (See Fig. 4.15)				
1. Too much	1. (a)	Lofting the ball.	1. (a)	See *lofting the ball.*
	(b)	Balance poor.	(b)	See *balance, poor* (3).
2. Too little	2. (a)	Bouncing ball.	2. (a)	See *ball release* and *dropping the ball.*
	(b)	Flipping ball.	(b)	See *flipping the ball.*
	(c)	No finger lift.	(c)	See *finger lift, poor* (2).
Foot turned (at foul line) (See Fig. 5.3)	1.	Foot turned in.	1 and 2.	Walk slower, shorten backswing, *roll* ball slower, do not force arm swing; also see *balance, poor.*
	2.	Ball pulled across body or no curve.		
	3.	Missed arrow.	3.	Keep head down and eyes on arrow.
Fouling	1.	Foot crosses line.	1 and 2.	Walk slower, take shorter first step, *roll* ball slower, balance over sliding foot, too little weight on slidfoot; also see *balance, poor.*
	2.	Hand touches over line, either floor, wall, or support.		
			2.	Keep body more upright, step back after ball is released, follow-through more.
High hit	1.	Hit head pin full.	1 and 2.	Move starting position two boards to inside, change hand position to 11 o'clock.
	2.	Chopping (cherry).		
	3.	Missing arrow.	3.	Concentrate on hitting arrow, head down.
	4.	Too much curve.	4.	See *ball release* (1).
	5.	Pulling the ball.	5.	See *pulling the ball.*
Hopping	1.	Hopping to the right (R.H.), to the left (L.H.) to maintain balance instead of sliding.	1.	Walk slower or faster, according to your present speed, keep body weight over sliding foot, keep arm swinging next to body, slide more, walk straight, maintain pendulum swing.
Light hit	1.	Continually hitting head pin lightly or not getting up to pin.	1.	Move starting position two boards to outside, change hand position to 9 o'clock, get more follow-through; see *ball release* (2).

Common Faults	Symptoms		Possible Remedies
	Missed arrow.	2.	Concentrate on arrow.
	No curve.	3.	See (1); also see *ball release* (2).
	Foot turned in	4.	See *foot turned*.
Lofting the ball (See Fig. 5.5)	Ball arcs through air, does not touch down smoothly, often sticks to thumb or fingers.	1.	Walk slower, reduce pushaway and arm swing, be sure ball fits correctly, holes not too tight, shorten *first step*, bend knee on sliding foot, bend lower at foul line.
Looking up (taking eyes off target) (See Figs. 4.16, 5.5)	Miss arrow.	1,2,3.	Concentrate on target arrow, walk slower, keep arm swing straight ahead, release ball properly, keep head down.
	Pull the ball.		
	No follow-through		
	Poor balance.	4.	See *blance, poor* (3).
Missed arrow	Looking up.	1,2,4,5.	Concentrate on arrow (many of the faults which occur may be eliminated or reduced by concentrating on the arrow); slow down.
	Eyes wander.		
	Throw too hard.		
	Missed pins.	3.	Reduce arm speed by reducing arm swing.
	Pulling the ball.		
	Walking wrong.	6.	Walk in a straight line, do not wander.
Pulling the ball	Arm across body.	1.	Caused by missing arrow, walking too fast, walking wrong, looking up.
	Missed arrow.	2.	See *missed arrow*.
	High hit.	3.	See *high hit*.
	Brooklyn hit.	4.	See *Brooklyn hit*.
Pushaway, poor (See Figs. 4.11, 4.13)	Timing poor.	1.	Push ball forward and down on first step, take short first step; see also *timing*.
	Release ball too soon, or late.	2.	Push ball more or less on first step.
	Balance poor.	3.	See (1,2); see also *balance, poor*.

Common Faults	Symptoms		Possible Remedies	
Sidewheeling (See Fig. 5.3)	1.	Ball behind back.	1.	Swing arm alongside body, keep body straight.
	2.	Float to one side.	2,3,4,5.	Walk straight ahead, stand erect, keep body square to foul line or target pin, *roll* ball slower; see (1).
	3.	Turning body.		
	4.	Wandering.		
	5.	Drifting.		
	6.	Turn foot in.	6.	See *foot turned.*
Throw too hard	1.	Ball goes too fast.	1.	Slow down, *roll,* do not throw, the ball.
	2.	Pins fly, not topple.	2.	Get more finger lift, flex fingers.
	3.	Foot turns in.	3 and 4.	See *foot turned in.*
	4.	Body turns away.		
	5.	No finger lift.	5.	See *ball release* (2,3,5,6).
	6.	Missed arrow.	6.	See *Missed arrow.*
	7.	Pulling the ball.	7.	See *pulling the ball.*
Timing, poor (See Figs. 5.3, 5.5)	1.	Walk too fast.	1.	Slow down, take short first step (this is the cause of most timing faults).
	2.	Body turns.	2,3.	See *foot turned in.*
	3.	Foot turns in.		
	4.	Pulling the ball.	4.	See *pulling the ball.*
	5.	Missed Arrow.	5.	See *missed arrow.*
	6.	Throw too hard.	6.	See *throw too hard.*
	7.	Foul.	7.	See *fouling.*
	8.	Long first step.	8.	Take short first step; see (1).
	9.	Pushaway poor.	9.	See *pushaway, poor.*
	10.	Backswing poor.	10.	See *backswing, poor.*
	11.	Ball release poor.	11.	See *ball release, poor.*
	12.	Balance poor.	12.	See *balance, poor.*

Common Faults	Symptoms	Possible Remedies
Twisting hand		
1. Hand turns to inside	1. (a) Ball spins and skids, little roll.	1. (a,b,c, d,e,f,g,h) Keep wrist straight and firm, follow through with arm alongside; see also *follow-through; timing, poor.*
	(b) Little curve.	(b) See *ball release (2,3,5,6); finger lift.*
	(c) Arm across body.	(c) See *pulling the ball.*
	(d) Topping the ball.	(d) Keep hand in proper release position.
	(e) Dropping the ball.	(e) See *dropping the ball.*
	(f) Ball seems to go off the side of hand.	(f) Do not twist your hand; see 1 (a).
	(g) Ball too fast.	(g) See *throw too hard.*
	(h) Turn the body.	(h) See *foot turned.*
2. Hand turns to outside (See Fig. 4.22)	2. (a) Back-up ball.	2. (a) See 1 (a) above; see also *ball release, poor.*
	(b) Body turns out.	(b) Keep body facing square to foul line or target pins, walk slower.
Walking		
1. Too fast	1. Body turns, throw ball too hard, miss arrow, not enough curve, foul, foot turns in, pins fly, ball is released too soon.	1. Slow down approach, take short first step, take shorter second step if needed, shorten approach distance, hold ball lower and shorten pushaway, roll the ball (do not throw); see also *ball release, poor,* and *timing, poor* (1).
2. Too slow	2. Too much curve, end too far from foul line, pins fall lazily, loft the ball.	2. Speed up your approach, longer pushaway, more backswing, lengthen approach distance, change from 4 step to 5 step approach.
3. Sidewheel and drift (See Figs. 5.2, 5.3)	3. End up too much to the right or left on lane, body turns.	3. See *sidewheeling.*

Finer Points of Bowling

As you become more proficient and gain self-confidence you will find there are some finer points of the game which may mean the difference between really being "a bowler" or being "just another" bowler. This chapter contains a discussion of such advanced techniques as playing the lanes, adjusting speeds, playing the angles, and analyzing your game.

Naturally, it is assumed that before any changes or alterations are made you have developed consistency in your game. A bowler who does not know what is going to happen as he bowls will not be able to make the adjustments necessary for better scoring.

PLAYING THE LANES

Hand Release Positions. Many bowlers fail to realize that at the moment the ball is released, the hand and fingers need to be in the correct position, slightly behind or on the side of the ball. What you do with your arm, wrist, or fingers before or after release does not help if your wrist is not straight (not flexed up or down, flipping, or cupped) and you do not generate any finger-lift to the ball, which naturally means a poor follow-through. There is a tendency to overcompensate when an adjustment is made.

One method of insuring proper wrist position at the release point is to hold the ball in the position in which you wish to release it as you assume the starting stance, and then maintain the position throughout the approach.

Some bowlers have natural wrist movements which may be advantageous (natural turn and lift), whereas others have a disadvantageous wrist movement (the back-up delivery common to most women bowlers). Forcefully imparting any unnecessary spin to the ball tends to increase control problems.

Too Much Curve. If you are getting too much curve or hook, and if the lane conditions are good and you are consistently rolling the ball smoothly, then you should check your hand-release position (thumb and fingers) at the point of release. Usually changing the thumb position closer to an 11 o'clock position will suffice, providing you do not overcompensate by imparting additional wrist and arm movement. Make doubly sure you are rolling the ball over the target arrow. Another adjustment which may help is to slightly increase the speed of your approach and/or arm swing. Adjustments may be made singly or in combinations. It is better to try them one at a time. If you wish to maintain the same curve, then moving your starting position three or four boards to the inside while continuing to use the same target arrow may work.

Too Little Curve. The common fault which causes too little curve is usually little or no finger-lift or too much speed imparted to the ball. Another common fault is not flexing the fingers when releasing the ball. Too little curve may be caused by fast lane conditions, which necessitates moving the starting position two to four boards to the outside of the normal position and continuing to use the same target arrow. Hand-release adjustments include moving the thumb position closer to 9 o'clock. Other possible solutions include a slower approach, shorter first step, more finger-lift, shorter backswing, and holding the ball nearer the waist when starting the approach. Make sure you are releasing the ball out on the lane and rolling the ball over the proper target arrow. Many faults are alleviated by rolling the ball over your target arrow.

Speed. As with automobiles, speed may kill your bowling scores. The correct speed is the key to successful bowling. Too much or too little speed generated during the approach, arm swing, or ball release usually jeopardizes your chances of continuous success. The correct speed allows the ball to work and causes the pins to fall. Obviously, every bowler will not use the same speed. The correct speed for you may be determined by observing the action of the pins. If the pins topple, rather than fly up or push straight back, you are on the way to good speed (providing you have not rolled the ball too slowly). A ball rolled too slowly is just as hard if not harder to control than a fast ball. Walking too fast to the foul line is the usual cause of too much speed imparted to the ball. Shortening the first step helps to slow the walk, and reduces the arm swing and pushaway motion. Of the remedies, shortening the first step will do wonders.

Lane Conditions. Although the ABC has standards for bowling establishments, different lanes within the same house often react differently. Each establishment may maintain its lanes as it sees fit. Some houses tend to score well on lanes and others score low, depending mainly on the way the lanes are maintained (surface dressing, and so on). Some lanes have almost human characteristics which seem to defy the management's attempts to make them into scoring lanes. Individual lanes tend to keep their individuality throughout their useful life. Remember how each lane *works* (reacts), as this will help you the next time those lanes are used.

The question arises, "What can we do about the situation?" To answer this, you must know how your ball works. An ideal situation is to know how your ball works on the best pair of lanes in your home house. This knowledge allows adjustments to be made on different lanes in relation to the home lanes.

Adjusting to fast or slow lanes was covered in the sections dealing with too much or too little curve. Adjusting to lanes with *slick* or *high boards* presents different problems. It seems that such lanes have their slick or high boards in the normal strike path. It is necessary in most cases to cross these boards one of two ways: (1) roll the ball so that the ball will *cross* the boards from outside in, or (2) roll the ball so that the path of the ball will cross the board going out and then swing back across the board. Another way of playing these lanes is to keep the path of the ball to the inside of the board, if there is room.

Some lanes have so-called *tracks* caused by surface wearing or poor lane maintenance. All lanes tend to *track* somewhat during each day as the surface dressing wears off, which is normal. One pleasant aspect of tracks is that if you can roll your ball so that it stays in the track, you should score well. If the track does not work for you, then an adjustment needs to be made similar to that for slick or high boards—cross the track or stay to the inside.

PLAYING THE ANGLES

One way most bowlers are able to improve their scores is to play the angles and/or percentage. The angles to play usually relate to spare angles. Although the basic spare angles were discussed in Chapter 5, you may wish to make some finer adjustments. The basic idea in playing the angles is to use as much of the lane width as possible. With this in mind, you normally need to move to the left when pins are standing on the right side of the lane, to the right for pins standing on the left side, and in the middle for pins termed middle lane spares.

Certain spare set-ups do not fall as readily when attempted from the basic angles. Fine adjustments need to be made to insure more success. In many cases an adjustment of one or even one-half of a board width to the right or left of your usual starting position may be the difference in picking an unusual set-up. Such a set-up is the 1−2−3−5, which normally would be a strike hit, but since it is not necessary to knock down the 4 or 6 pins, for instance, you could move one or two boards to the right (R.H.) or left (L.H.) of the usual strike position. By moving to the outside your ball should hit higher in the pocket, with less chance of leaving the 5 pin or hitting too thin, which may leave the 2 or 3 pin, depending on whether you are right- or left-handed. Other spares more common are the 4−7 or 6−10 pin leaves, which can be made by using the same spare angle as that used when attempting either the 4 or 7 pin, or the 6 or 10 pin. There is a good chance of a cherry when using either of the basic spare angles for the 4−7 or 6−10 pin leaves, so to alleviate this possibility, move about two boards to the outside of your normal 4 or 6 pin spare position, which permits your ball to cover both pins. (See Figs. 4.36, 4.38, 4.42.)

The bucket (2−4−5−8 for right-handers, 3−5−6−9 for left-handers) is another spare that many bowlers prefer to try at an angle other than the 2 or 3 pin angles. Those using a different angle prefer to move to the far left side (L.H.) or far right side (R.H.) and roll the ball over the third arrow from the right side (L.H.) or left side (R.H.). (See Figs. 4.40, 4.48.)

As you become proficient in ball control and bowling strategy, you may want to experiment with other angles. Above all, be sure you know exactly what you plan to do before the ball is rolled.

Figure 6.1 1−2−3−5 spare.

ANALYZING YOUR GAME

Many bowlers fail to pay attention to their own game; that is, they never seem to know where to stand, how to roll the ball, which arrow to look at, or how fast the ball should travel. These bowlers seldom do very well and are usually the ones who feel the other bowlers are always lucky and get the breaks. Admittedly, you will not always be able to do exactly what you plan, but chances are better if you have a plan than if you trust to plain luck. Luck or the breaks normally occur to those who perform well and have a plan of attack. Leave nothing to chance. As many bowlers say, "I didn't throw the ball badly, the pins just fell strangely." It is much better to explain why the pins fell than why they didn't fall.

You may analyze your own game either with or without help. If someone can observe you bowling, the observer should be told exactly what you intend to accomplish; try the maneuver to see if the execution was as planned. As you make your delivery have the observer watch the exact path of the ball, where the ball touches down, if the ball goes over the target arrow, how the pins fall, finger position when releasing the ball, arm swing and follow-through, position of the sliding foot, and body position at the foul line upon completion of the delivery. During the approach, such items as the pushaway, length of steps, and walking speed need to be checked. If you have problems with any of these phases refer to Chapter 5 for possible remedies.

A self-analysis method is to maintain a record of the pins left standing after each ball has been rolled. It is also desirable to record where the pins are hit by each ball. After you have bowled ten or more games, make a recapitulation by tallying each different pin leave in a game and noting whether you made the spares, including the types of splits and whether they were picked. If, on the first ball, you are consistently missing the head pin or getting *light hits*, move your starting position two to four boards to the outside of your usual starting position. If you are continually coming in *high* move your starting position two to four boards to the inside of the usual starting position. Be doubly sure you are getting the proper finger-lift as the ball is released.

A majority of bowlers tend to become overly concerned about their bowling scores when practicing. When you practice, be sure you *practice*; forget about the score. Practicing may be done in one of two ways for effectiveness: (1) *shadow ball* if the lanes are so equipped; or (2) try to pick certain pins from a full rack, such as the 10 pin, and then use the second ball to roll from your strike position. The *shadow ball* method is useful because there are no pins to worry about knocking down, so you tend to concentrate on the arrow and hand release position, as well as approach and pushaway. If you must keep track of the frames used, then merely mark each frame used with a big *X* and concentrate on what you have planned.

DIAGNOSTIC QUIZ

1. How do you play a *fast* lane? *slow* lane?
2. How do you change the amount of *curve* or *hook* on your ball?
3. Does the speed of your ball affect pin action?
4. What is a *high board* and how do you play it?
5. Why play the angles when shooting at spares?
6. Can you analyze your own game?
7. What advantages are there in using *shadow balls?*

League
Bowling

7

One of the greatest aspects of bowling is becoming a member of a team which bowls in a league and tournaments. Teams usually have five members, although some leagues have two-, three-, or four-member teams. Teams may be composed of all men, all women, or both (mixed). Leagues may have as few as 4 teams or as many as 40. The majority of leagues are composed of 6 to 24 teams. Leagues which have both men and women team members are classified as mixed leagues.

HANDICAP AND SCRATCH LEAGUES

Of the several designations for leagues, the most popular are the handicap and scratch leagues. The beauty of handicap leagues is that each bowler competes on the same relative level as each other bowler. Almost all leagues require a team to play three games during each league session. Leagues with fewer than five members on a team often bowl four games during a series. With automatic pinspotters, leagues are able to function any time of the day or night. There are even leagues which bowl after the midnight hour.

League and tournament bowling involves bowling on a minimum of two lanes during a series. This is done by alternating lanes (bowl one frame on a lane, then switch to the other lane). This alternation is easily accomplished, as each team member follows the previous team member in the same order as the lineup shows. The team listed on the left-hand or top of the score sheet bowls the first frame of the first game on the odd-numbered lane, with the opponents beginning on the even-numbered lane. After the first frame the leadoff bowler follows the anchor man of the opponents, then teammates follow in the regular order. In this manner each team member alternates lanes throughout the game. Each succeeding game begins on the same lane where the tenth frame was bowled in the previous game.

BOWLING ORGANIZATIONS

The ABC, WIBC, and AJBC govern league and tournament play for men, women, boys, and girls. These organizations set the rules and regulations, but they are in turn governed by the bowlers themselves through national conventions. Each organization furnishes the supplies for league officers and team captains and also furnishes various achievement awards for high games, league champions, 300 games, and so on.

TOURNAMENT BOWLING

The most famous tournament in bowling is the ABC annual championships, which attract more than 5,000 teams and 30,000 men bowlers. This tournament is the largest sports participant tournament in the world. Although the WIBC annual tournament is not as large as the ABC, it is the largest women's participant tournament in the world. There are many other tournaments for bowlers, ranging from the local city association to state and regional tourneys. Prize money may range from $25.00 to $25,000 for an event. The ABC often has total prize monies in excess of $500,000 to be won.

Each city bowling association must have a tournament each year for only the local association members. Both the men and women have separate bowling associations, even though several men and women are members of mixed leagues.

Most tournaments in which you will probably participate are of the handicap variety. That is, your team, doubles, and singles final scores are determined by including a handicap with your game scores in each event. All events are usually computed from the scratch scores.

Practically all tournament winners are determined by bowling only three games in each event. The final standings are determined by the rank order of the three game totals.

LEAGUE BOWLING

As previously mentioned, leagues are the backbone of bowling. League championships are normally determined by the number of games a team wins and loses. A common variation is to allow an extra point to the team which outscores its opponent in the series (usually based on the non-handicap total, but not necessarily). The basis for using a four-point won/lost system is to keep players from sandbagging (deliberately bowling poorly). Team games which end in a tie count as a half-game won and a half-game lost. In handicap leagues, wins and losses are determined by adding the handicap to the team's scratch score for a final team handicapped score. Scratch team winners are determined by the total of the actual scores bowled by each team member.

Computing League Averages

If you bowled games of 140, 135, 164, 172, 102, and 125, what would be your per-game average? Each bowler in a league has an average, which is computed by adding all of the league games together and dividing the total pins by the actual number of games bowled. Have you computed the average of the games listed? If not, do it now. Total pins = __ ÷ number of games __ = __ average. Did you total 838 pins? There are 6 games, so 838 ÷ 6 = 139 average. *In bowling, all fractions are dropped, whether in computing league averages or handicaps.* In this case the fractional average is 139.66, although you would be credited with only a 139 average. The importance of the league average cannot be overemphasized. The league average reflects how well or poorly you are bowling. (Refer to Chapter 3, goals.)

In an informal study of league bowling averages, Robert Showers discovered an interesting method for determining an average for a bowler in a league in which the league average per man is around the 190 level. The formula is: 199 + (percent of games over 199 minus 50 percent) = ±2 pins of the bowlers final average. In the case of the author's average, 199 + (51/96 - 50 percent) = 199 + (53% - 50%) = 199 + 3 = 202. Actual final average was 201.6 for the season.

Team Lineup (Strategy)

The makeup of a team (lineup) can be very important. The ideal method is to have your highest average players bowl either in the leadoff or anchorman position. Usually the highest average man is placed last, second highest average bowls first, lowest average second, middle average third, and the third highest average bowls fourth. Many teams do not have any particular order, but those teams that do seem to perform better if there is some logical reasoning (much the same as a baseball team).

Many teams have an extra player on the team. The best method of utilizing all players is to have a rotation plan whereby one man does not bowl each week (each player has a night off) according to a predetermined schedule. This method permits emergency lineup changes in the event a scheduled player is unable to bowl. Some teams use a system in which the extra player who sits out is the one who has the lowest series score for that league session. The problem with the latter method is that one or two players may do almost all of the sitting out, although it does provide for additional competition, even if among one's own team members.

It is often important to find out in which position a player prefers to bowl. Some players do not bowl well in either leadoff or anchorman positions, regardless of what their averages may be, whereas some bowlers have a hard time following certain teammates. The team captain has the responsibility for making a team lineup. Once a game has started, players are not permitted to change the lineup order. However, lineup order changes may be made prior to each game. Substitutions may be made at any time during a game or series. The player who starts a game is credited with the score of that game if a player substitution is made after the first frame of the game.

As in most sports, there is an advantage to player positions as well as to finishing on an even- or odd-numbered lane. The bowler on the right has the right-of-way if two players are ready to bowl at the same time. This could be important in a close game when the anchormen bowl (determining who should go first).

Some phases of bowling involving leagues may or may not be followed in tournaments or when practicing.

Joining a League. Individuals or full teams wishing to join a league should contact their local bowling establishments for possible openings. Individuals are often needed to fill existing teams within a league. Single teams may have difficulty getting into an existing league, whereas several teams could form a league and have more of an opportunity to bowl.

Restrictions. Many leagues have certain restrictions, such as: all men, all women, or mixed; membership in a club, work group, or church, beginners' leagues, minimum average leagues (usually scratch leagues), or maximum average leagues (usually handicap leagues). Each league has its own governing rules and regulations in addition to the rules of the ABC, WIBC, or AJBC.

League Fees and Prizes. In general, bowling establishments require leagues to have guaranteed fees (all bowling fees must be paid—even for absent members). This is only fair to the establishment because, in a sense, the lanes are being rented for a specified time to a league. Practically all leagues have a prize fee in addition to the bowling fee, which is used to defray the costs of operating the league. Leagues pay a sanctioning fee to the national organization and local city association, secretarial fees, and trophy costs. Money which is left over is distributed to the teams and individuals as prize money. Prize funds of most leagues are rather small except for a top-notch league like a scratch league. High school students or below are not permitted to bowl in leagues or tournaments in which prize money is returned, under penalty of losing their amateur standing.

Handicap Leagues. Handicap leagues are the most popular. As the name implies, a handicap is given to the lowest average team or individual as a means of equalizing competition. In this way, bowlers of all ages and sexes may compete on nearly an equal basis.

Briefly, handicaps are computed by taking the differences between the averages of two teams, and multiplying by the league's predetermined handicap percentage (usually 75 percent). In closed leagues, such as a club, a higher percentage may be used, and in leagues where small differences exist between teams a lower percentage may be used. Individual handicaps are figured in the same way as those for teams.

Computing a Handicap. To illustrate, assume that the author's team (1,008 average) is to bowl a team with an average of 727.

Author's team	1,008	(team average)
Opponent	− 727	(opponent's team average)
	281	(difference between averages)
	.75	(75 percent handicap)
	210.75	(product–handicap)
	210	pins handicap per game

The total number of pins handicap per game would be 210 (all fractions are dropped). This means that the author's team would have to outscore the opponent by 211 pins to win.

The same principle is applied if two individuals are to play each other. As an illustration, suppose George bowled Dick.

George	210	(individual average)
Dick	−135	(individual average)
	75	(pins difference)
	.75	(75 percent handicap)
	56.25	product—pins handicap per game

Thus, Dick would receive 56 pins per game handicap. George would have to outscore Dick by 57 pins to win a game, or by 169 pins to win a three-game series.

Another method of handicapping that is becoming more popular is the predetermined handicap for each bowler. Each player has a handicap that is then added together to form a team handicap with the difference between the two teams being the actual handicap. This type of handicap is based on an average which is higher than anyone in a particular league, usually figured from 180 or 200. Using the 200 average figure, and a team with individual averages of 180, 170, 160, 150, and 140, the respective predetermined handicaps would be (based on 75 percent of the difference between 200 and the bowler's average) 15 + 22 + 30 + 37 + 45 for a team total of 149. The advantage of this method is that there are fewer computing errors as only the league secretary has to determine the handicaps.

Scratch Leagues (nonhandicap). Scratch leagues (no handicap is permitted) are usually reserved for the high-average bowlers. Scratch leagues are for men, women, or in some cases are mixed. They generally employ some kind of a minimum average rule (players must maintain at least a certain average or have a certain average before being permitted to bowl). There are leagues which have an upper limit for team averages (team members may have any averages providing the total does not exceed league limit). Scratch leagues are generally prestigious. An example would be the *Bowl Haven Lanes Classic League,* Alton, Illinois, of which the author's team, *International Dairy Queen,* is a past league champion. Players with high averages (over 180) usually prefer bowling in scratch leagues.

Marks

A running tally is kept of all *marks* made by each team during a game. A mark is allowed for each strike or spare made by each team member providing certain basics are met. In general each mark is worth 10 pins. In Figure 7.1, the team has 7 good marks at the end of the fourth frame. If this team were playing another which had 4 marks at the end of the fourth frame, there would be approximately 30 pins difference between the team scores at the end of the fourth frame (7 - 4 = 3 ; 3 x 10 = 30). What are the basic rules to follow in figuring marks?

1. 1 mark is given for each *single* strike or spare.

2. 2 marks are given for each *consecutive* strike.

3. *Lost marks*—a mark is lost for a team if an individual fails to knock over *at least* 5 pins:

   (a)   with the *first* ball following a spare.
   (b)   with the *first* ball following a multiple strike.
   (c)   with *both* balls in a frame (total less than 5).
   (d)   with *both* balls following a strike (total less than 5).

Thus, it is possible for a team to have negative marks in the first frame or any frame after; also, an individual may lose 2 marks in a single frame (such as bowler C in Fig. 7.1). The reasoning behind a *lost mark* is that two players could have the same number of strikes and spares, yet the player who has not lost any marks might be 20–30 pins ahead.

In the illustrative game involving three players (Fig. 7.1), notice the first frame. Players A and C both made spares and B got a strike, for a total of 3 marks in the first frame. In the second frame several things happened. First, A only knocked down 3 pins with the first ball, so, in accordance with rule 3a above, he *loses* his mark in the first frame, which reduces the 3 to 2 marks. Player B strikes again for a double, which counts as 2 marks (see rule 2 above). Player C performs as A did, getting only 2 pins on the first ball and losing the first frame mark, which now reduces the 2 to 1 mark for the first frame; but since C failed to get 5 pins or more total in the second frame, a mark is also lost in the second frame (see 3c). Total marks at the end of the second frame are now 2 (1 left in first frame plus 2 - 1 in the second frame). Notice players A and C—after two frames they have 20 and 15, plus each having made a spare. A player could have as high as 18 for two frames without a mark, and would be ahead of C but behind A. When a player fails to keep a mark it is termed a *lost mark*, whereas marks that are not lost are called *good marks*.

All players strike in the third frame. Players A and C each get credit for 1 mark and player B receives 2 more marks for an additional consecutive strike, which totals 4 marks $(1 + 2 + 1 = 4)$ for the third frame and, when added to the second frame total of 2 makes a grand total of 6 marks at the end of the third frame.

Player A strikes in the fourth frame, which counts as 2 marks. Player B knocked down one pin with the first ball in the fourth frame, which according to rule 3b *loses* one of the two marks B had in the third frame, thereby reducing the teams 6 marks to 5 marks for the third frame. Player B then fails to score on the second ball and totals only one pin for the fourth frame, which *loses* a mark in the fourth frame in accordance with rule 3d. Even though the pin total is less than 5 and meets the lost mark requirement in both rules 3c and 3d, only one additional mark is lost in this instance. Player C knocked down only 3 pins with the first ball; however, no mark is lost, since two balls are allowed on a strike (see 3d). Player C picks the spare for an additional mark, which makes a total of 2 marks for the fourth frame $(2 - 1 + 1 = 2)$ and makes a grand total of 7 marks (5 in third frame plus 2 in fourth frame) at the end of the fourth frame.

In the tenth frame, marks are counted a little differently as shown in Fig. 7.2. Not all possible combinations are shown but the five rules for counting in the tenth frame are covered.

a. Regular spare in tenth frame counts as one mark (Fig. 7.2, player A).

b. First ball strike in the tenth frame, with no strike in ninth frame, counts as one mark (Fig. 7.2, player B).

c. First ball multiple strike in the tenth frame, with a strike in ninth frame, counts as two marks (Fig. 7.2, players C and E).

d. Second ball multiple strike in the tenth frame counts as one additional mark (Fig. 7.2, players C and D).

e. Last ball strikes or spares in the tenth frame are not counted as additional marks (Fig. 7.2, players A, D, and E).

Generally marks are not counted in the tenth frame since you already know what the various scores are for each team. Remember, keeping track of the marks does not alter any player's or team's score. Marks are only used as a guide to keep tab on which team is winning without adding all of the subtotals each frame. If one team has consistently higher *pin count* on their spares and multiple strikes as well as

Figure 7.1 Can you compute the number of marks?

Player	1 _____ 1 2	2 _____ 1 2	3 _____ 1 2	4 _____ 1 2
A	9 ⊘	3 4	✗	₂ ✗
B	✗	₂ ✗	₂ ⊗	① —
C	6 ⊘	② ①	✗	3 ⁄
Total Marks	3⁄ 2 1	2 (1+1)	∅ 5 (2+4) (−1)	7 (5+2) (3−1=2)

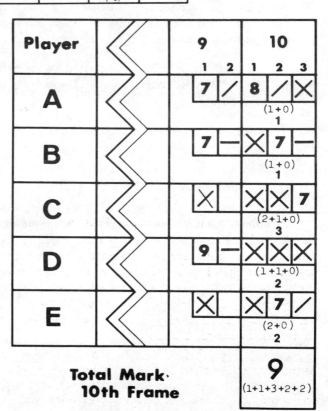

Player			9 ___ 1 2	10 _____ 1 2 3
A			7 ⁄	8 ⁄ ✗ (1+0) 1
B			7 —	✗ 7 — (1+0) 1
C			✗	✗ ✗ 7 (2+1+0) 3
D			9 —	✗ ✗ ✗ (1+1+0) 2
E			✗	✗ 7 ⁄ (2+0) 2

Total Mark 10th Frame

9 (1+1+3+2+2)

Figure 7.2

total pins in a frame, team final scores may easily vary from 10 to 50 pins, even though the final mark total may be even; one team can be ahead in marks and lose the game because of pin count (rather like baseball, the team with the most hits may not always win, but their chances are better).

Team Scores. The final team results are scored on a cumulative basis. That is, the second player's score is added to the first, third score to the second, fourth to third, and fifth to the fourth score, thereby ending up with a team total rather than waiting until the last bowler has finished to add the totals together. As illustrated in the table the *correct method* produces a running score or cumulative team total showing the progress of the game, whereas in the *poor method* you need to wait until the game is over in order to tell who won.

| | Correct Method | | | Poor Method | |
Player	10th Frame	Total Score	Player	10th Frame	Total Score
A	161	—	F	152	152
B	145	306	G	141	141
C	171	477	H	135	135
D	185	662	I	167	167
E	201	863	J	181	181
					776

After each game has been completed, the team captains should enter each individual's score on the special team summary score sheet. Fewer errors are made if the scores are recorded after each game. As soon as the series has concluded, all individual series totals need to be computed and then cross-checked against the team totals (the time to correct mistakes is at the time they occur, not the following week). Team captains should also sign the final team summary sheet. A team summary of three games is shown here as a guide.

In the sample final team summary, notice that the team won two games and lost one game. If this league used the 4 point system (1 point for each win plus 1 point for series total pins), then this team has won 2 points and lost 2 points (one game lost plus series total).

Sample Team Summary

Player	Game 1	Game 2	Game 3	Series Total
A	161	144	151	456
B	145	122	125	392
C	171	180	140	491
D	185	152	147	484
E	201	167	173	541
Scratch total	863	765	736	2364
Team hdcp.	210	210	210	630
Grand total	1073	975	946	2994

Games Won: 2   Lost: 1
Points Won: 2   Lost: 2

League Champions. League winners are determined by a number of methods. One of the most common is to divide the season into two parts, called *halves*, with each *half* winner meeting in a best of five games *roll-off* for the league championship. Another popular way is similar, except the season is divided into four parts, called *quarters*, and the quarter winners have a play-off, pairing the winners of quarters one and two, and three and four; these winners then play for the league championship. The third general method is to decide according to the total games a team wins and loses during the season. The advantage of either half or quarter system is that it allows a team to get a fresh start rather than suffer through a full season after a bad start.

Many leagues employ a position round at the end of each half or quarter, whether or not the league has a split season. This method permits those teams to bowl each other which are in a challenging position (team in first plays second team, third plays fourth, and so on).

Some leagues have what is called a sweeper after the regular season is completed. A sweeper is a closed tourney open only to the members of a particular league. Winners are determined according to a team score, singles, and blind doubles (names picked at random). An individual's three-game series counts in all three events.

Estimating a Score

It is possible to estimate your final score without re-adding the line score. It is the responsibility of each bowler to know what his score is and to correct any mistakes.

The quick way of estimating is to count all of your *good, live* marks, multiply the total by 10, and add 90. Unless you had poor pin count your final score should be within a few pins of the estimate. Refer to the illustrated score in Chapter 3. Notice there are 8 *good, live marks* (the last spare in tenth frame is a *dead* spare). Using the above formula: 8 marks x 10 + 90 = 80 + 90 = 170. Final score was 162, a difference of 8 pins. As you analyze the score, notice the 7 pin count in the first frame, which is a 2 pin count *loss* (based on 9 pins per frame), plus 1 pin in the fourth frame, plus 1 pin in the fifth, a 2 pin loss on the first ball in the seventh and an additional 2 pin loss on the second ball, plus a 2 pin loss on the second ball in the tenth frame, making a total of 10 pins lost in pin count by one player. Instead of the bowler having a game of slightly over 170, the game was 162. Pin count is important.

A minimum of 11 marks is needed to score a 200 game, with one exception—a *dutch* 200 game has 10 marks. A minimum of 53 to 55 marks is needed for a five-man team to have a 1,000 score. If an individual or a team has very few strikes, then additional marks are usually needed to attain the scores mentioned.

SPECIAL RULES

There are many rules with which you ought to become familiar that may be found in any current ABC, WIBC, or AJBC rules book. Covered here are a few that are often overlooked.

1. **Bowling on the Wrong Lane.** Players bowling on the wrong lane must nullify their score for that frame and bowl on the proper lane. If both teams have bowled complete frames on a wrong lane they must bowl an additional frame on that lane, then bowl two consecutive frames on the other lane before alternating lanes.

2. **Ball Leaving the Bowling Lane.** Any pins knocked down by a ball that bounces out of the channel or pit must be respotted. Pins knocked down by other pins that leave the lane are legally knocked down. Pins that fall over and then stand up again are *not* counted as knocked down.

3. **Sandbagging.** Bowlers who deliberately bowl in a manner to keep their averages low or who falsify their league average are subject to dismissal with a suspended sentence, for a specified length of time, or indefinitely.

4. **Pinsetter Knocking Pins Over.** Any pins knocked down or touched in the act of falling by the pinsetter must be respotted on their original spot. This usually occurs when a pin has been moved off spot so far that the pinsetter cannot pick up the pin properly. One bowler had 11 strikes in a row, threw a bad twelfth ball, and missed the head pin. However, pins began falling, and finally the headpin was hit by another pin and started to fall when the automatic pinsetter touched the pin, picked it up, and respotted the pin, which then proceeded to fall over. The bowler did not receive credit for a 300 game—rules are rules, and must be obeyed.

5. **Fouling.** Many bowlers do not realize that even though the automatic foul light does not register when you foul, the foul must be counted and recorded. Team captains are vested with this responsibility.

   (a) **Deliberate Fouls.** Bowlers who deliberately foul to gain an advantage are subject to immediate dismissal from the game, and possibly dismissal for an indefinite time.

   (b) **Unusual Fouls.** Most fouls occur when a bowler's foot or feet go beyond the foul line. Other fouls that sometimes go unnoticed or unrecorded are:

   (1) Touching a wall or post beyond the foul line.
   (2) Fouling on an adjoining lane (usually caused by a player losing balance or swinging the non-sliding foot around and to the side).

The basic rule to follow is—do not let any part of your person touch anything beyond the foul line (if something falls from a pocket make sure you let a player know you are going to pick up the object).

DIAGNOSTIC QUIZ

1. What is league bowling?
2. What are the men and women's national governing organizations?
3. What are the differences between league and tournament bowling?
4. What is a league average and how do you compute an average?
5. Is there a method to determine a team's line up?
6. What is the difference between a handicap and a scratch league?

7. How do you compute a handicap?

8. What are *marks* and how do you figure them?

9. How do you record team results?

10. How are league championships determined?

11. Is there a short cut method to estimate you score?

12. What are some of the special rules in bowling?

13. What is sandbagging?

Bowling
Customs

Bowling has certain customs and etiquette which may be written or unwritten. These range from using your own ball to not talking to a bowler who is ready to bowl. Bowling customs involve nothing more than being polite to your fellow players.

There are many ways to show your knowledge of these customs. Congratulating another player on a job well done, even though he may be your opponent, helps to keep a desirable atmosphere for both you and your opponents. Knowing who and when to razz or cheer may be rewarded by good bowling. It is normally in poor taste to volunteer advice unless the person asks or you know he will not resent advice.

DO'S AND DON'TS

1. **Whose Turn?** Always be ready to bowl when it is your turn. There are players who make a habit of seldom being ready for their turn, usually being late for the match, not knowing on which lane to bowl, or not being able to find their ball. (See Fig. 8.1).

2. **Who Shoots First?** When two players are ready to bowl at the same time, custom dictates that the bowler on the right has preference. If a left-handed person is involved, he goes first. Usually if a player is trying for a spare and the bowler on the right is attempting a strike, and both bowlers are ready, let the spare shooter go first. Observation studies show

that a player who is attempting a strike will take up to twice as much time as one who is attempting to pick a spare. (See Fig. 8.2.)

Figure 8.1 Be ready when it's your turn to bowl.

Figure 8.2 Don't walk ahead of a player who is ready to bowl.

3. **No Talking.** (See Fig. 8.3.)
4. **Use Your Own Equipment.** (See Fig. 8.4.)
5. **Stay on Your Own Approach.** (See Fig. 8.5.)
6. **Do Not Foul.**
7. **Wait Your Turn.** (See Fig. 8.6.)
8. **Do Not Blame the Equipment.**
9. **Call Pins by Number (Not Names).** (See Fig. 8.7.)
10. **Make Sure the Pins Are Ready.** (See Fig. 8.9.)
11. **Refrain From Using Foreign Substances on Equipment.**
12. **Make Sure No Liquids Are on Your Shoes.**
13. **Do Not Loft the Ball.** (See Fig. 5.5.)
14. **Picking Up the Ball.** (See Fig. 8.8.)
15. **Be Careful of Practice Swings.** (See Fig. 8.10.)
16. **Exhibit Good Sportsmanship.**

Figure 8.3 Don't talk to a player ready to bowl.

Figure 8.4 Use your own ball.

Figure 8.5 Stay on your own approach.

Figure 8.6 Wait your turn.

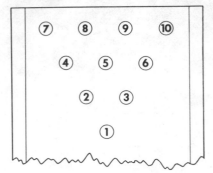

Figure 8.7 Call pins by number.

Figure 8.8 Pay attention when you get your ball.

Figure 8.9 Make sure the pins are ready.

Figure 8.10 Be careful of practice swings.

Outstanding Accomplishments

Many excellent accomplishments have been done over the years since the ABC was organized in 1895, and the WIBC in 1916. Following are listed some of the greatest performances that have occurred in sanctioned league or tournament play unless otherwise noted.

300 Games
First in ABC Leagues: Earnest Fosberg, East Rockford, Ill., 1902.
First in ABC Tournament: Billy Knox, Toledo, Ohio, 1913.
First in WIBC Leagues: Mrs. Charlene Fahning, Buffalo, N.Y., 1929-30.
First in AJBC Leagues: Fred Chase, Chicago, Ill., 1952.
First 2-Consecutive: Frank Caruana, Buffalo, N.Y., 1924.
First 2-Consecutive (nonsanctioned): Clarence Brayshaw, Peoria, Ill., 1906.
First 3-Consecutive (nonsanctioned) Leo Bently, Lorain, Ohio, 1931.
First on TV: Graz Castellano, New York, N.Y., 1953.
Most in Lifetime: (Man) Elvin Mesger, Sullivan, Mo., 24. (Women) Sylvia Wene Martin, Philadelphia, Pa., 3.
Most in One Year: Elvin Mesger, Sullivan, Mo., 8.

800 Series (3 games)
First on TV: Buzz Fazio, Detroit, Mich., (802), 1955.
Most in Lifetime: Elvin Mesger, Sullivan, Mo., 20
Most in One Year: Elvin Mesger, Sullivan, Mo., 6.

Highest League Averages
Men: 238, Skang, Mercurio, Cleveland, Ohio, 1934-35. 238 Bob Pinkalla, Milwaukee, Wisc., 1959-60. 238, Mike Durbin, Chagrin Falls, Ohio, 1971-72.
Women: 219, Mildred Martorella, Rochester, N.Y., 1967-68.

Highest League Series (3 games)
Men: 886, Allie Brandt, Lockport, N.Y., 1939 (297, 289, 300). 890, (unofficial) Ray Orf, St. Louis, Mo., 1972 (290, 300, 300). 853, (lefthanded bowler) Bruce Blindman, Minneapolis, Minn., 1962.
Women: 818, Beverly Ortner, Galva, Iowa, 1968-69. 737, (WIBC tournament) D. D. Jacobson, Playa Del Ray, Calif., 1972.
Boys: 847, Wayne Chester, Daly City, Calif., 1969.
Girls: 737, Dana Stewart, San Carlos, Calif., 1971.

Highest Team Series (5-member)
Men: 3858, Budweiser, St. Louis, Mo., 1958.
Women: 3379, Freeway Washer & Stamping, Cleveland, Ohio, 1959.

Highest Team Game (5-member)
Men: 1342, Hook Grip Five, Lodi, N.J., 1950.
Women: 1193, Pitch's Lounge, Milwaukee, Wisc., 1965.

All-Events (9 games)
Men: 2259, Frank Benkovic, Milwaukee, Wisc., 1932. 2235, Tom Ryan, Zanesville, Ohio, 1972. 2227, Clyde Potter, Akron, Ohio, 1940.
Women: 2101, Dorothy Feathergill, N. Attleboro, Mass. 2093, Betty Kuczynski, Chicago, Illinois, 1972. 2028, Olga Gloor, Chicago, Ill.

Miscellaneous Records
Most Strikes (3 games): 35, Ray Orf, St. Louis, Mo., 1972
Most Spares (consecutive): 30 Howard P. Glover, San Francisco, 1944. 30, Charley Claybaugh, Anderson, Ind., 1952.
Most 700 Series (women): 24, Mildred Mortorella, Rochester, N.Y.
Most Team Losses (0-120): Downs Construction, Moravia, N.Y., 1965-66.
Most Bowling Lanes: Japan, 252 lanes. United States 116 lanes, Willow Grove Park Lanes, Willow Grove, Pa.

Suggested Readings

American Bowling Congress. *History of Bowling.* Milwaukee, Wisconsin: American Bowling Congress, 1959.

Rules and Regulations. Milwaukee, Wisconsin: American Bowling Congress, current printing.

American Machine and Foundry (AMF). *Bowling Instructor's Manual.* 1962.

Bellisimo, Lou. *The Bowler's Manual.* Englewood Cliffs, N.J.: Prentice-Hall, 1969.

Brunswick Advisory Staff. *The Secrets of the Stars.* Chicago, Illinois: Brunswick-Balke-Collender Company, 1959.

Fraley, Oscar. *The Complete Handbook of Bowling.* Englewood Cliffs, N.J.: Prentice-Hall, 1958.

Miller, Donna Mae, and Katherine Ley. *Individual and Team Sports for Women.* Englewood Cliffs, N.J.: Prentice-Hall, 1955.

Showers, Norman E. "A Study of Certain Factors Affecting Bowling Performance." Master's thesis, University of Southern California, 1951.

Showers, Norman E., and Gerber, Richard. "A Statistical Analysis of Men and Women League Bowling Scores," Illinois Journal of Health, Physical Education and Recreation, Fall 1969, p. 6. Jacksonville, Illinois: Production Press. Also published in the 73rd Annual Proceedings of the National College Physical Education Association for Men, December 1969.

Showers, Robert G. "A Study of Certain Factors Affecting Bowling Performance of Female Bowlers." Master's thesis, University of Southern California, 1953.

League Rule Book. Columbus, Ohio: Women's International Bowling Congress, Inc., current printing.

Student/Teacher
Instructional Objectives

Comments on the Use of the Student/Teacher Evaluation Forms

The forms which follow were designed to be used in a variety of instructional settings. Preplanning and organization are necessary for these devices to be used as effectively as possible. The purpose of evaluation is for gauging how well the course objectives are accomplished. That is, evaluation will indicate the progress and the extent to which learning has occurred.

Although the learner *must do his own learning*, the teacher's role is to guide and to direct learning experiences and to provide for appropriate measurement procedures. The charts which follow have been constructed to place primary responsibility on the individual student for estimating progress and indicating areas which need work. It may not be either necessary or desirable to use all the materials provided here in a given teaching learning situation. The instructor and the student should work together to select the materials most appropriate for the course.

It must be remembered that sufficient time for practice and study must be provided if the individual is to perfect his skills as well to accrue knowledge and to develop understanding. The time available may not be adequate for *all* students to demonstrate acceptable levels of skill performance. The instructor may wish to supplement the evaluation devices with a written test covering analysis of performance, procedures, and rules. (Sample tests will be available in a separate instructor's manual covering the entire Goodyear Physical Activities series.) The written test provides an opportunity for the student to demonstrate his knowledge and understanding of the skill even though his actual skill might be less than desired. Final evaluation for grading purposes should take into account a number of variables which may have an influence on individual performance.

STUDENT	BOWLING BALL	TEACHER
	Weight	
	Span	
	Grip	
	Regular	
	Semi-Finger Tip	
	Finger-tip	

BODY STARTING POSITION

Hand Position

STUDENT		TEACHER
	Hand Shake	
	Palm Up	
	Hand Turned Out	
	Hand Turned Down	

Wrist Position

	Wrist and Arm form straight line	
	Wrist Bent In	
	Wrist Bent Out	
	Ball Cupped In Hand	

Ball Position (Where Held)

	Near Waist High	
	Shoulder High	
	Chest High	
	Below Waist (low)	
	Ball Held Next To Body	
	Ball Held Away From Body	

Body Stance

	Straight (Not Tense)	
	Straight (Tense)	
	Leaning Forward	
	Leaning Back	

Class _____

Student _____

Teacher _____

Date _____

STUDENT		TEACHER
_____	Leaning To Side	_____
_____	Knees Bent	_____
_____	Body Bent At Waist	_____

Body Balance

_____	Equal On Both Feet	_____
_____	Mostly On One Foot	_____
_____	One Foot On Floor, Other Foot With Heel Raised	_____

Foot Position

(Right Foot, RH; Left Foot, LH)

_____	Foot lined up straight to correct starting position	_____
_____	Foot at an angle to starting position	_____
_____	Not lined up with correct starting position	

APPROACH TO FOUL LINE

Number of Steps

_____	4 or 5 steps	_____
_____	3 steps	_____
_____	Other	_____

Foot Movement

_____	Start with correct foot	_____
_____	Start with opposite foot	_____
_____	First step is short	_____
_____	First step is long	_____
_____	Feet kept in contact with the floor (shuffle)	_____
_____	Feet leave floor (walking style)	_____

Class _____

Student _____

Teacher _____

Date _____

STUDENT		TEACHER
_____	Walk is steady, medium speed	_____
_____	Walk is fast	_____
_____	Walk is slow	_____
_____	Walk is unsteady, jerky	
_____	Walking direction is in straight line	_____
_____	Walking direction is zig-zag style	_____
_____	Walking direction is to the side	_____

Eye Position

STUDENT		TEACHER
_____	Eyes focus on correct target arrow	_____
_____	Eyes focus on target pins	_____
_____	Eyes do not focus on any particular object	_____

Ball Pushaway

STUDENT		TEACHER
_____	Move ball forward and down	_____
_____	Move ball up and forward	_____
_____	Move ball directly down and to side	_____
_____	Move ball directly to the rear	_____

BODY MOVEMENT

Starting

STUDENT		TEACHER
_____	Ball and foot start at same time	_____
_____	Ball starts first, then foot	_____
_____	Foot starts first, then ball	_____
_____	Ball held for one or more steps	_____

Class _____

Student _____

Teacher _____

Date _____

STUDENT · **During Approach** · TEACHER

Body gradually
lowers and upper
body leans
forward

_____   _____

Body remains
rather straight

_____   _____

Body bends for-
ward at the waist

_____   _____

Body leans
backward

_____   _____

Arm Swing (With Ball)

Arm is relaxed
and straight

_____   _____

Arm is bent
at elbow

_____   _____

Arm is straight
and tense (rigid)

_____   _____

Arm swings out
(to side) from
body

_____   _____

Very little arm
swing motion

_____   _____

Balance Arm (Arm Without Ball)

Arm away from
body for balance

_____   _____

Arm stays in
front of body

_____   _____

Arm remains
across body

_____   _____

Arm makes
contact with
sliding leg

_____   _____

Shoulder Position

Shoulder drops
normally and is
square to foul
line

_____   _____

Shoulder is
forcefully
dropped (lean)

_____   _____

Shoulder is turned
to rear (body
turned)

_____   _____

Class _____

Student _____

Teacher _____

Date _____

STUDENT		TEACHER
	## Head Position	
_____	Head steady and eyes looking at proper arrow	_____
_____	Head moving and little eye-arrow coordination	_____
_____	Head bent forward at neck and down	_____
_____	Head straight and tilting backward	_____

BODY AT THE FOUL LINE

FOOT POSITION

STUDENT		TEACHER
_____	Sliding foot is left foot (right hander)	_____
_____	Sliding foot is right foot (left hander)	_____

Sliding Foot

STUDENT		TEACHER
_____	Straight and pointed toward target	_____
_____	Turned inward	_____
_____	Turned outward	_____
_____	Distance from foul line from 1" - 6"	_____
_____	Distance from foul line more than 6"	_____
_____	Foot goes over foul line	_____

BODY POSITION

STUDENT		TEACHER
_____	Sliding leg bent at knee	_____
_____	Sliding leg knee straight (little bend)	_____
_____	Non-sliding foot is to the rear and off floor	_____
_____	Non-sliding foot has toes touching lightly	_____
_____	Non-sliding foot has weight being supported	_____

Class _____

Student _____

Teacher _____

Date _____

STUDENT	Upper Body	TEACHER
_____	Straight and leaning forward from waist	_____
_____	Straight and very little lean forward	_____
_____	Bent (hunched) at waist	_____
_____	Leaning backward	_____
_____	Body balanced at foul line on sliding foot	_____
_____	Body leans to the side	_____
_____	Body leans to the rear	_____
_____	Body twists or turns at foul line	_____
_____	Slide is smooth and controlled	_____
_____	Slide is forced	_____
_____	Slide is non-existant	_____

EYE POSITION

_____	Eyes looking at target arrow	_____
_____	Eyes looking at the pins	_____
_____	Eyes not looking at any particular target	_____

Hand Release Position
and Follow Through

_____	Hand shake position	_____
_____	Palm facing up	_____
_____	Palm turned outward	_____
_____	Palm turned under (facing down)	_____
_____	Fingers bent in palm (middle two fingers)	_____

Class _____

Student _____

Teacher _____

Date _____

STUDENT		TEACHER
_____	Fingers straight	_____
_____	Wrist relatively straight with inside of arm	_____
_____	Wrist bent forward	_____
_____	Wrist bent backwards	_____
_____	Wrist cupped	_____
_____	Arm swing forward and up	_____
_____	Arm swings across body (even small amount)	_____
_____	Arm stays down to side (little movement)	_____

BALL DELIVERY

STUDENT		TEACHER
_____	Hook ball	_____
_____	Curve ball	_____
_____	Back-up (reverse curve)	_____
_____	Straight ball	_____
_____	Ball spins on axis and goes straight	_____
_____	Ball rotates backward	_____
_____	Ball is not delivered in a consistant manner	_____

LANE ADJUSTMENT

STUDENT		TEACHER
_____	Makes adjustments for fast (slick) lanes	_____
_____	Makes adjustments for slow (running) lanes	_____
_____	Makes adjustments to fast center and slow edges	_____
_____	Makes adjustments to slow center and fast edges	_____

Class_____

Student_____

Teacher_____

Date_____